T0271011

SYSTEMS
DESIGN

Shingo Model Series

Discover Excellence
Edited by Gerhard Plenert (2017)

Enterprise Alignment and Results
Edited by Chris Butterworth (2019)

Continuous Improvement
Edited by Larry Anderson, Dan Fleming, Bruce Hamilton &
Pat Wardwell (2021)

SYSTEMS
DESIGN
BUILDING SYSTEMS THAT DRIVE IDEAL BEHAVIOR

Edited by
Brent R. Allen and April A. Bosworth

Routledge
Taylor & Francis Group

A PRODUCTIVITY PRESS BOOK

First published 2022
by Routledge
605 Third Avenue, New York, NY 10158

and by Routledge
2 Park Square, Milton Park, Abingdon, Oxon, OX14 4RN

Routledge is an imprint of the Taylor & Francis Group, an informa business

ISBN: 978-1-032-21310-1 (hbk)
ISBN: 978-1-032-22935-5 (pbk)
ISBN: 978-1-003-16776-8 (ebk)

DOI: 10.4324/9781003267768

Typeset in Minion
by Deanta Global Publishing Services, Chennai, India

To the leaders at Lifetime Products,

who always showed the courage to improve.

Contents

Editors

Brent R. Allen recently retired after 38 years of service from Lifetime Products, a leading manufacturer in outdoor basketball equipment, folding tables and chairs, outdoor storage, playground equipment, kayaks, and coolers in Clearfield, Utah. Brent was hired in 1981 as the general manager of American Playworld, a sister company to Lifetime. At that time there were 11 employees. By the end of 2018, Lifetime had 3,000 employees. Brent was a special education teacher before working at Lifetime and American Playworld. He earned a degree in psychology and education at Weber State University. Brent has been happily married for 45 years and enjoys all forms of outdoor activity such as hiking, kayaking, and riding ATVs. Brent worked closely with Shaun Barker to create the highly successful Shingo SYSTEM DESIGN workshop.

April A. Bosworth is a writer specializing in educational and informational topics. She has written about business, art history, yoga, nursing, software applications, and banking regulations. She currently teaches writing to adults learning English at the English Language Center of Cache Valley, Utah.

Acknowledgments

This book is based on a two-day SYSTEMS DESIGN workshop presented by the Shingo Institute. Shawn Barker, assistant executive director of the Shingo Institute, and Brent R. Allen are the co-authors of this workshop. Shawn was part of the original Shingo Institute team that created the *Shingo Model* in 2008. His contribution to the SYSTEMS DESIGN workshop and the development of the *Shingo Model* cannot be overstated. Ken Snyder, executive director of the Shingo Institute, has provided excellent guidance to both the creation of the book and the workshop. Shingo Institute Client and Affiliate Manager Amy Sadler's professionalism and support were invaluable.

Several of the Shingo Institute affiliates were willing to teach the workshop while it was still in development. Larry Anderson and Dan Fleming from GBMP and Drew Butler from HKPO deserve our thanks for being willing to be pioneers in teaching the workshop.

Much of the thought that has gone into this book is the result of thinking done by leaders at Lifetime Products, including David Winter, Richard Hendrickson, Denise Wandling, Ted Esplin, and Roger Mulholand. The editors would like to acknowledge the work done by this group.

The case studies are an important part of this book as well. Nathan McConkie told the Lifetime Products story. Dave Siebert and Tolan Brown explained how O.C. Tanner was implementing System Design in their company.

Special thanks to the staff at the Shingo Institute, particularly Ken Snyder, Shaun Barker, Amy Sadler, Mary Price, and Jennifer Payne for keeping the project moving forward and offering much appreciated guidance. We are grateful to Nedra Allen who provided moral support, an excellent eye for detail, and a superb sense of audience. We also want to thank everyone who participated in the Shingo Institute SYSTEMS DESIGN Workshop in 2019. We appreciate your willingness to help us improve and your insight into the subject of System Design.

Brent R. Allen
April A. Bosworth

Introduction

The ground-breaking *Shingo Model* of 2008 introduced principles, systems, tools, and results that would help an organization achieve excellence. At the time, however, the systems element of the model did not receive the in-depth attention that other parts of the model did. As a result, organizations have developed their own concept of the meaning of systems. Some organizations have identified literally hundreds of systems and tools. In fact, the distinction between a system and a tool has not been clearly defined until recently, with the introduction of the SYSTEMS DESIGN workshop and the publication of this book.

Robert "Bob" Miller was executive director of the Shingo Institute at the time the new model was published. In his book, *Hearing the Voice of the Shingo Principles*, Bob offers this definition of a system: "A system is a complex network of tools or activities that are highly integrated to accomplish a shared objective."* He gives an analogy of an early version of a smart phone being a system and the keyboard being a tool:

> *An example of the relationship between systems and tools may help. To the complex systems we call a smart phone, the keypad is a tool. It is a specific thing that enables the system. But a key pad is also a system, enabled by a tool called a touch key, which is in itself a complex system and so on and so on. Actually, the smart phone is just a tool to enable a complex system of information management, and so it goes.†*

In an attempt to define Miller's "so it goes," consider the systems and components as shown in Table 0.1. The smart phone analogy is a good way to recognize the relationship between a tool and a system. But the analogy

---

* This is a paraphrase of W. Edwards Deming's definition of a system: "A system is a network of interdependent components that work together to try to accomplish the aim of the system." See William Edwards Deming, *The New Economics: For Industry, Government, Education* (Cambridge, MA: MIT Press, 2000), 50.
† Robert Miller, *Hearing the Voice of the Shingo Principles: Creating Sustainable Cultures of Enterprise Excellence* (New York, NY: Routledge, 2018), 60.

A Variety of Systems	
System	**Components**
Touch key	Plastic cover with letter on it, spring, electrical connection
Key pad	All of the touch keys
Mobile phone	Key pad, screen, microphone, power source, case, computer chips
Audible Communication Devices	Mobile phone, desk phone, radios
Communication devices	Audible communication devices, desktop computers, fax machines
Information management	Desktop computers, servers, networks
Administration	Information management, human resources, legal
Organization	Administration, operations/production, sales/customer relations, supply, finance

TABLE 0.1

An expansion of Miller's example of systems shows how a broad definition of "system" can be confusing

also illustrates the confusion that is found in many organizations of what is meant by a system.

In 2008, the Shingo Institute planted a stake in the intellectual ground* of organizational improvement when it introduced the *Shingo Model* with its ten guiding principles and the ideal behaviors that support them. The *Shingo Model* and its guiding principles have served many organizations around the world well for more than a decade. (Read more about the development of the *Shingo Model* in Chapter 1 of this book.)

In the intervening years, the *Shingo Model* has continued to develop. In 2012, the Shingo Institute provided further guidance to the *Shingo Model* by identifying three types of systems: the work system, the improvement system, and the management system. Work systems are organization units that work together for a common output. Examples of work systems could be shipping, maintenance, and packaging. The improvement system functions to make the organization better. Examples of improvement systems would be problem-solving, idea generation, and training.

---

* Staking the corners of a piece of property to identify the land claimed is a time-honored tradition that still functions in modern mineral claims. Land could be claimed for mineral rights by marking the corners of the property with a stake driven into the ground and registering the claim.

Management systems develop system leaders. Examples of management systems may include administration, production, and supply.

A few years later in 2019, Shingo Institute asked Brent R. Allen to assist in the creation of a SYSTEMS DESIGN workshop. The bulk of the thinking on systems within the *Shingo Model* came from the work of developing the workshop. The claim (the stake in the ground) that the Shingo Institute is making now, with the publication of this book and the SYSTEMS DESIGN workshop, is the formal introduction of the three essential systems and the five required tools, among other necessary components, that add depth and breadth to the model designed with the intent to help organizations achieve excellence (Figure 0.1).

Two organizations also had a hand in helping bring about the SYSTEMS DESIGN workshop and this book. Brent R. Allen, lead editor of this book, was executive vice president of operations at Lifetime Products from 1986 to 2018. Lifetime Products is a leading manufacturer of residential basketball systems, utility tables, storage sheds, kayaks, swing sets, and coolers. In 2012, Lifetime Products was privileged to have the Shingo Institute teach the *Shingo Model* to the leaders of the company. While the managers at Lifetime were thrilled with the teachings of principles, tools, and results, they were unsure of what to make of systems. The leaders of Lifetime took on the challenge to develop their own understanding of systems. They put extensive work into defining work systems, improvement systems, and management systems.

FIGURE 0.1
Mineral claim boundaries can be marked by driving a labeled stake into each corner of the property.

More recently, in 2019, O.C. Tanner played a critical role in the development of the Shingo SYSTEMS DESIGN workshop. With 1,600 employees, O.C. Tanner develops strategic employee recognition and reward solutions that help people accomplish and appreciate great work. As a winner of the Shingo Prize in 1999, they have been working on systems for years. O.C. Tanner hosted the developmental phases of the SYSTEMS DESIGN workshop. Their input and questions have greatly clarified the content you will find in this book.

The purpose of *Systems Design: Building Systems that Drive Ideal Behavior* is to formalize the process of creating work, improvement, and management systems. In addition, a new tool, the system design map, is introduced. This book will also clarify how to improve the connections between the tools, systems, results, and principles of the *Shingo Model.*

1

Organizational Excellence and the Shingo Institute

> Too many organizations are failing to be competitive, not because they cannot solve problems, but because they cannot sustain the solution. They haven't realized that tradition supersedes tools, no matter how good they are. Success requires a sustainable shift in behaviors and culture, and that needs to be driven by a shift in the systems that motivate those behaviors.*
>
> —*Gerhard Plenert*

In 1988, Shigeo Shingo, a Japanese industrial engineering consultant and author, bestowed his name on the "North American Shingo Prizes for Excellence in Manufacturing." While recognized for his genius by only a few individuals in the West, Shingo was highly regarded in Japan as a co-creator of the concepts, tools, and philosophy of the Toyota Production System (TPS). He was also the author of 18 books on the subject (Figure 1.1).

Vernon Buehler, a director of Utah State University's (USU) Partners in Business program, was an early advocate of Shingo's teachings. It was Buehler who persuaded Shingo to accept an honorary doctorate in 1988 and to add his name to the Prize for Excellence in Manufacturing.

Shingo wanted the prizes, which were administered by the Jon M. Huntsman School of Business at Utah State University, to be awarded each year to organizations and academics whose work exemplified the best of Shingo's teachings. The prizes were to be awarded in three categories: (1)

---

* Gerhard Plenert, *Discover Excellence: An Overview of the Shingo Model and Its Guiding Principles* (Boca Raton, FL: CRC Press, 2018), 1.

DOI: 10.4324/9781003267768-1

1

FIGURE 1.1
Shigeo Shingo receives an honorary
doctorate at Utah State University in
Logan, Utah, in 1988.

large businesses of more than 500 employees, (2) small businesses of 500
or fewer employees, and (3) academics who made scholarly contributions
to the body of knowledge surrounding Shingo's work.

The mission of the Shingo Prize was, as it is today, to recognize the
successful implementation of Shingo's ideas as examples of best practices
for others to follow. Shingo wanted "to give back to North America" for
what he himself had learned from his "teacher's teachers." These included
Frank and Lillian Gilbreth, William Taylor, and Henry Ford.

With a $50,000 donation from Norman Bodek, founder and former
president of Productivity Press, and generous support from USU, the
fledgling Shingo Prize presented its first award in 1989 at the 14th Annual
Partners in Business Conference in Logan, Utah. By that time, several
of Shingo's books had been translated into English from Japanese. This
afforded organizations throughout the world the benefit of his incredible
tools, such as SMED (single-minute exchange of dies) and poka-yoke
(mistake proofing). Perhaps even more valuable in Shingo's teachings were
his observations on human nature and development, although the latter
points were largely overlooked in favor of his tools in the early days of the
Shingo Prize.

By 2008, Shingo's work and the significance of TPS beyond
manufacturing became apparent to the Shingo Prize administrators.
They expanded the scope of the Shingo Prize beyond North America and
also made the Prize available to participants from non-manufacturing

entities. The rebranded "Shingo Prize for Operational Excellence" was adopted. It included two additional significant but lesser levels of the award: the silver and bronze medallions. Around this time, Prize administrators recognized the need and responsibility to provide a deeper understanding of the conceptual and philosophical foundations of Shingo's tools and methods, the *know-why* behind the *know-how*, as Shingo described them in his teachings.

BACK TO BASICS

The term *Lean* was first introduced in 1990 in the book *The Machine That Changed the World: The Story of Lean Production*. In it, the authors, James Womack, Daniel Jones, and Daniel Roos, describe Lean as manufacturing systems that are based on the principles employed in the Toyota Production System (TPS). They wrote:

> *Lean ... is "lean" because it uses less of everything compared with mass production—half the human effort in the factory, half the manufacturing space, half the investment in tools, half the engineering hours to develop a new product in half the time. Also, it requires keeping far less than half the inventory on site, results in many fewer defects, and produces a greater and ever-growing variety of products.**

In the intervening years, the philosophy of Lean has gone through numerous iterations. It stresses the maximization of customer value while simultaneously minimizing waste. The goal of Lean is to create increased value for customers while simultaneously utilizing fewer resources. Countless organizations have, at one time or another, begun a Lean journey or implemented an improvement initiative of some sort. At the foundation of these initiatives are a plethora of tools (over 100) that seem to promise exciting new results. They are utilized to optimize the

---

* Womack, J. P. et al. *The Machine That Changed the World: The Story of Lean Production—Toyota's Secret Weapon in the Global Car Wars That Is Now Revolutionizing World Industry* (New York, NY: Simon & Schuster, Inc., 1990), 14.

flow of products and services throughout an entire value stream as they horizontally flow through an organization.

While many organizations may initially see significant improvements, far too many of these initiatives meet disappointing ends. Leaders quickly find that tools such as Six Sigma, SMED, 5S, and JIT are not independently capable of effecting lasting change.

THE SHINGO INSTITUTE

The Shingo Institute has assessed organizations in various industries around the world. The Institute has seen firsthand how some organizations have been able to sustain their improvement results, while far too many have experienced such a decline. In fact, initially, the Shingo Prize focused on tools and systems and how those tools and systems drive results. The Prize was originally given out based on these results.

But when far too many Shingo Prize recipient organizations reverted to their old ways, the Shingo Institute realized there was a big piece missing in its earlier model of organizational excellence based only on systems, tools, and short-term results. So, the Shingo Institute set out to determine the key difference between short-lived successes and sustainable results. Over time, the Institute discovered a common theme: the difference between sustainable and unsustainable effort is centered on the ability of an organization to ingrain into its culture timeless and universal principles, rather than rely on the superficial implementation of tools and programs. This is because principles help people understand the "why" behind the "how" and the "what." Sustainable results depend upon the degree to which an organization's culture is aligned to specific, guiding principles rather than depending solely on tools, programs, or initiatives.

The Shingo Institute discovered that what was lacking was sustained superior performance, a sustained culture of excellence and innovation, and a sustained environment for social and ecological leadership. To really make progress in a journey to organizational excellence, we must have long-term sustainability. Change could no longer be something that happened once a year during a Lean event. Instead, organizations need to constantly look for improvement opportunities.

THE SHINGO MODEL AND THE SHINGO PRIZE

To best illustrate its new findings, the Shingo Institute developed the *Shingo Model*™, the accompanying *Shingo Guiding Principles*, and the *Three Insights of Organizational Excellence*™. The principles are timeless and universal. They apply to all cultures and they do not change over time. They govern consequences and provide a solid foundation for developing a roadmap to excellence.

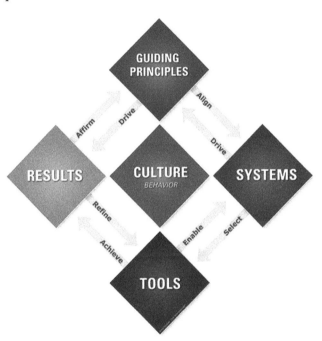

Now, the Shingo Prize is awarded to organizations that have robust key systems driving behavior closer to ideal, as informed by the principles of organizational excellence, and measured by strong key performance indicator and key behavioral indicator trends and levels. Shingo Prize recipients show the greatest potential for sustainability as measured by the frequency, intensity, duration, scope, and role of the behaviors evident in the organizational culture. The Shingo Prize has become the global standard for organizational excellence. As an effective way to benchmark progress toward excellence, organizations throughout the world may apply and challenge for the Prize. Recipients receiving this recognition fall into three categories: Shingo Prize, the Shingo Silver Medallion, and the Shingo Bronze Medallion.

Most organizations do not wait until they believe they might qualify for the Shingo Prize to challenge for it. They challenge for the Prize so they can have a team of organizational excellence experts visit their company and evaluate their performance. They use the *Shingo Model* and the assessment process to measure themselves as they work toward the highest standard of excellence in the world. They use the guidelines to direct them, to inspire them, and to hold themselves responsible.

Over the years, the Shingo Institute's scope has expanded to include various educational offerings, a focus on research, and a growing international network of Shingo Licensed Affiliates. The *Shingo Model* is the primary subject of the Institute's popular workshops and publications. These materials have been developed to share throughout the world so organizations can learn how to create a sustainable cultural shift, which will ultimately lead to organizational excellence.

Similarly, volunteer Shingo examiners, who are international experts in all aspects of organizational excellence, focus on determining the degree to which the *Shingo Guiding Principles* are evident in the behavior of every team member in an organization. They observe behavior and the evidence of it to determine the frequency, intensity, duration, scope, and role of current behavior measured against the desired principle-based behaviors. They observe the degree to which leaders are focused on principles and culture, and the degree to which managers are focused on aligning systems to drive ideal behaviors at all levels.

THE SIX SHINGO WORKSHOPS

As part of its educational offerings, the Shingo Institute offers a series of six workshops that are designed to help participants understand the *Shingo Model*, its guiding principles, and its insights. Ultimately, these workshops help participants strive for excellence within their respective organizations. Each of the workshops is described below.

DISCOVER EXCELLENCE

This foundational, two-day workshop introduces the *Shingo Model*, the *Shingo Guiding Principles*, and the *Three Insights of Organizational Excellence*. With active discussions and on-site learning at a host organization, this program is a highly interactive experience. It is designed to make learning meaningful and immediately applicable as participants discover how to release the latent potential in an organization to achieve organizational excellence. It provides the basic understanding needed in all Shingo workshops; therefore, it is a prerequisite to all the other Shingo workshops. During this workshop, participants will learn and understand the *Shingo Model*, discover the *Three Insights of Organizational Excellence*, and explore how the *Shingo Guiding Principles* inform ideal behaviors that ultimately lead to sustainable results. They will also understand the behavioral assessment process through an interactive case study and on-site learning.

SYSTEMS DESIGN

This two-day workshop integrates classroom and on-site experiences at a host facility to build upon the knowledge and experience gained in the DISCOVER workshop and focuses on the Systems and Tools diamonds in the *Shingo Model*. It begins by explaining that all work in an organization is the outcome of a system. Systems must be designed to create a specific end objective; otherwise, they evolve on their own. Systems drive the behavior of people, and variation in behavior leads to variation in results. Organizational excellence requires well-designed systems to drive ideal behaviors that are required to produce sustainable results. During this workshop, participants will discover three types of essential systems and explore five required communication tools for each system. They will also learn how to create and use system maps and understand system standard work and how it drives improvement.

CULTURAL ENABLERS

This two-day workshop integrates classroom and on-site experiences at a host facility to build upon the knowledge and experience gained in the DISCOVER and SYSTEMS workshops. It takes participants deeper into the *Shingo Model* by focusing on the principles identified in the Cultural Enablers dimension: Respect Every Individual and Lead with Humility.

Cultural Enablers principles make it possible for people in an organization to engage in the transformation journey, progress in their understanding, and build a culture of organizational excellence. Organizational excellence cannot be achieved through top-down directives or piecemeal implementation of tools. It requires a widespread organizational commitment. The Cultural Enablers workshop will help participants define ideal behaviors and the systems that drive those behaviors using behavioral benchmarks.

CONTINUOUS IMPROVEMENT

This two- or three-day workshop integrates classroom and on-site experiences at a host facility to build upon the knowledge and experience gained in the DISCOVER and SYSTEMS workshops. It begins by teaching participants how to clearly define value through the eyes of their customers.

It continues the discussion about ideal behaviors, fundamental purpose, and behavioral benchmarks and takes participants deeper into the *Shingo Model* by focusing on the principles identified in the Continuous Improvement dimension: Seek Perfection, Embrace Scientific Thinking, Focus on Process, Assure Quality at the Source, and Improve Flow & Pull. The CONTINUOUS IMPROVEMENT workshop will deepen participants' understanding of the relationship between behaviors, systems, and principles and how they drive results.

ENTERPRISE ALIGNMENT

This two-day workshop integrates classroom and on-site experiences at a host facility to build upon the knowledge and experience gained in the DISCOVER and SYSTEMS workshops. It takes participants deeper into the *Shingo Model* by focusing on the principles identified in the Enterprise Alignment dimension: Think Systemically, Create Constancy of Purpose, and Create Value for the Customer.

To succeed, organizations must develop management systems that align work and behaviors with principles and direction in ways that are simple, comprehensive, actionable, and standardized. Organizations must get results. Creating value for customers is ultimately accomplished through the effective alignment of every value stream in an organization. The ENTERPRISE ALIGNMENT workshop continues the discussion around defining ideal behaviors and the systems that drive them.

BUILD EXCELLENCE

This two-day capstone workshop integrates classroom and on-site experiences at a host facility to solidify the knowledge and experience gained from the previous five Shingo workshops. The BUILD EXCELLENCE workshop demonstrates the integrated execution of systems that drive behavior toward the ideal as informed by the principles in the *Shingo Model*. The workshop helps to develop a structured approach to execute a cultural transformation. It builds upon a foundation of principles, using tools that already exist within many organizations. Participants will learn how to build systems that drive behavior that will consistently deliver desired results.

In this final Shingo workshop, participants will learn how to design or create a system, guided by the *Shingo Model*, that changes behaviors to close gaps and drives results closer to organizational goals and purpose. They will answer the question: "How do I get everyone on board?" They will understand the relationship between behaviors, systems, and principles, and how they drive results. Finally, participants will learn how KBIs drive KPIs, and how this leads to excellent results.

THE SHINGO MODEL SERIES OF BOOKS

In conjunction with the Shingo Workshop series, the Shingo Institute has set out to publish six books that are specifically focused on the primary components of the *Shingo Model* and its guiding principles. This book, *Systems Design*, is one of the books in the series. Three others, *Continuous Improvement, Discover Excellence*, and *Enterprise Alignment*, have already been published and the others are on the horizon.

In all of these efforts, the focus at the Shingo Institute is unique in the world. Its work is the most rigorous way to determine if an organization is fundamentally improving over the long term. Its goal is to help every organization reach excellence—wherever it may be along its path.

2

Systems Overview

Organizations design systems with the intent of achieving specific results, and they select tools to support those systems.[*]

— ***Shingo Institute***

INTRODUCTION TO SYSTEMS

The scope of a system can be as big as the universe or as small as a gas pump. In an organization, systems are generally created one by one without regard for each other. Because each unit in an organization works to optimize itself, these internal systems are often independent and do not fit well together. The systems thinking described in this book will introduce you to a method for identifying existing systems, connecting existing components into systems, and aligning those systems. The *Shingo Model* teaches, *"All work in organizations is the outcome of a system. Systems must be designed to produce a specific end goal, otherwise they evolve on their own."*[†]

CURRENT STATE OF SYSTEM THINKING

In the past, Shingo Institute trainings have offered this definition of a system: *A system is a collection of tools working together to accomplish an intended outcome.*[‡] This definition allows for a very broad

---

[*] Shingo Institute, *The Shingo Model*, version 14.6 (Logan, UT: Utah State University, 2021), 7.
[†] Shingo Institute, *The Shingo Model*, 15.
[‡] Shingo Institute, *The Shingo Model*, 8.

DOI: 10.4324/9781003267768-2

understanding of what a system is. When using the broad definition of systems, programs, plans, structures, processes, teams, and strategies are all systems. Table 2.1 illustrates the wide variety of possible systems under this broad definition.

The term *system* is used in many ways. The dictionary gives 6 definitions of systems that encompass 14 different types of systems*: The first definition, which is the most relevant to our purposes here, states: "A group of interacting, interrelated, or interdependent elements forming a complex whole." Following are examples of systems that are mentioned in the dictionary:

Excretory system
Root system
Heating system
Highway system
Computer system
Philosophical system
Feudal system
Taxonomy system
Metric system
Returned merchandise system (method)
Cave system
Weather system
Restaurant kitchen system
"Can't beat the system" (social order)

Other common, recognizable systems are the postal system, transportation system, school system, even the New England Patriots offensive system.

With so many different uses for the term *system*, you may conclude that there can be a lot of different ideas about what a system is. The Systems diamond in the *Shingo Model* focuses specifically on the systems found in a business organization.

---

* *The American Heritage Dictionary of the English Language*, 5th ed., s.v. "system."

Example		Collection of Tools	Intended Outcome
Program	Company-wide donation drive for United Way	Posters Emails Video training from United Way Personal HR visits to each area to request funds Record of money coming in Donations end and issue check to United Way Thank you cards to all donors	Donate to United Way
Plan	Vacation	Questions and research: budget, location, travel mode, length Proposal and consensus: Disneyland–3 days, beach–1 day, drive–2 days. Total: 6 days	Enjoy family time together
Structure	Organizational Chart	President 4 VPs: Operation, Finance, HR, Supply Chain 25 department heads 75 supervisors 1,000 employees	People work together to have a successful company
Process	Spray paint parts	1-Receive the part, 2-Clean the part, 3-Hang the part, 4-Gather spraying material and paint, 5-Ensure the right paint for the spray gun, 6-Mix the paint, 7-Load the spray gun, 8-Spray the part, 9-Check the paint coverage, 10-Empty/clean part	Paint a part
Team	Cross functional recognition team	Meet once per month Representatives from all areas of the company Budget: $5,000	Create a proposal for the executive team to better recognize people
Strategy	Corporate Strategy	1-Mission statement 2-Vision 3-Company values 4-Goals and measures	Make the company successful

TABLE 2.1

Possible systems according to the collection of tools definition. Can you identify a system using this definition?

READER CHALLENGE

Take a moment to identify five systems in your organization.

1. _____

2. _____

3. _____

4. _____

5. _____

The current state of thinking about systems gives a definition that is too broad and leaves each individual to define systems on their own. Peter Senge, a senior lecturer at the MIT Sloane School of Management, founded the Society for Organizational Learning, and wrote *The Fifth Discipline: The Art and Practice of the Learning Organization*. He shared his perspectives on systems thinking at a lecture at IBM in 2014.

The term systems thinking is really a mixed bag and I use it very, very cautiously. First, both words are problematic but ... system is the most problematic, because if you say the word "system" ... the image that pops up into most people's head is [a] computer system. ... The second most common association is [a] management control system. As [in], it's not my fault, it's the stupid system. ... Neither of them is what we're trying to help people understand.

So, whenever I'm trying to help people understand what this word "system" means, I usually start off by saying, "Are you part of a family?" Everybody is part of a family. Have you ever seen people producing consequences in the family that aren't ... what anybody intends? How does that happen? ... People can tell their stories and think about it. That, then, grounds people in—not the jargon ... systems thinking— but the reality that we live in webs of interdependence.

A family is fairly close-knit. You can see most all of the key players. ... We can identify ... ten or fifteen names; here's all the key people in my immediate family. ... The complexity of interactions amongst all those people is obviously such that, consistently, families produce outcomes that nobody wants.

The other fundamental rationale for all of this [is] not to understand systems. That's an abstraction. It's to understand how it is that the problems that are the most vexing, difficult, and intransigent that we all deal with come about. … A perspective on those problems … gives us some leverage and some insight as to what we might do differently.*

As Senge points out, even the word *system* is problematic. He gives an excellent example of the family being a system. In a family, it can be easy to see people producing unintended consequences. "The complexity of the interactions" of the people in a family "produce outcomes that no one wants."

DEFINITION OF A SYSTEM

For the purposes of this book, we will take our definition of a system from W. Edwards Deming who is best known for his pioneering work in the 1950s in Japan where he taught methods for improving how top managers and engineers worked and learned together.† His contribution to systems thinking is based on his books *Out of the Crisis* and *The New Economics for Industry, Government, Education*. A respected thinker in the field of quality management, Deming gives us this definition of a system: "A system is a *network of interdependent components* that work together to try to accomplish *the aim* of the system."‡

Components

According to Deming, the key to understanding a system is to understand how each component of a system connects to the other components. In order to understand a system, we must first understand all the components of a system. Removal of a component has an impact on the system as a

---

* Kris Wile, "Peter Senge Introduction to Systems Thinking," August 5, 2014, video, 2:20, https:// www.youtube.com/watch?v=eXdzKBWDraM.
† The W. Edwards Deming Institute, "Deming the Man," accessed February 11, 2021, https://deming .org/deming-the-man/.
‡ William Edwards Deming, *The New Economics: For Industry, Government, Education* (Cambridge, MA: MIT Press, 2000), 50. Emphasis added.

whole. Many organizations have clearly defined the components of work systems. Most organizations also have a management system, though the leaders are generally defined by their place in the organization rather than their connections to the work systems. Fewer organizations have a consistently implemented company-wide integrated improvement system. As your system's vision becomes clear and focused, you will see the ways in which tightly connected systems will support a culture of excellence within your organization.

Consider the ecosystem, which is a commonly understood system. An ecosystem is made up of the atmosphere, sun, land, water, plants, bugs, animals, and much more. All of the components of the system are necessary for the system to function properly and remain in balance. If something goes askew with the bugs, all of the other components will be affected. This is true in an organization as well.

Interdependence and Network

A system is not merely the components. Dr. Deming emphasized the connections among each of the components with the words *network* and *interdependent*. Consider your list of systems in your organization. Are they working well together, or are they working independently? When identifying organizational systems, many people think first of a process, a manufacturing line, or a department, such as purchasing. But your organization is much more than just a few processes, departments, or lines.

It may be helpful to consider a more complex natural example of a system: the human body. The body itself is a system which, like your organization, encompasses many sub-systems including circulatory, digestive, respiratory, and nervous. Each of those body sub-systems is itself a system of components. For example, the digestive system includes the teeth, the stomach, and the intestines. A successful organization is likely to have many different systems and sub-systems, such as accounting, manufacturing, and shipping. In fact, all of the work of an organization is produced by a system. When the key systems of an organization aim at the same target of sustainable excellence using the same communication tools, the bonds of interdependence strengthen, creating (or supporting) a tight-knit, sustainable culture.

Ideally, by making clear decisions about how to organize the components into specific systems and about how to connect the systems with solid, tight, strong connections, your organization will support the culture of excellence you are striving for.

As an example of the need for networked connection, consider problem-solving in your organization. Problem-solving tools should be used consistently across the entire organization. But are they? Can you identify the leader responsible for problem-solving across the organization? Is there standard work for problem-solving? Is there consistent problem-solving training? Most organizations have problem-solving tools but they are missing the vital connections that make these tools effective. It is likely that your organization has many of the components of improvement systems but they are not networked and interdependent.

Aim

Deming chose the word *aim* instead of *goal* or *target*. It is not enough to have a target. It is important that members of a system all aim at or are aligned with the target. In shooting sports, taking aim is essential to hitting the target. In most companies, there is no shortage of goals or targets. But there is a lack of good shots that consistently hit the target. When shooting an arrow, it is not enough to have perfect technique; you must also aim carefully at the target and make necessary adjustments to your efforts until your arrow arrives consistently in the center of the target. In an effort as complex as your organization, it is essential that every person knows the direction to face, the distance to pull the bow, and the moment to release the arrow.

As the definition of a system shifts from a loose, general definition (informal) to a tight, specific one (formal), the connections through the organizational culture (especially those that are missing) come into focus. When applying the principles of the *Shingo Model*, it becomes possible to improve the culture of the organization by improving the connection between the systems, tools, results, and principles of the organization.

INFORMAL VERSUS FORMAL SYSTEMS

With a definition of a system at hand, consider Figure 2.1. Is the pile of rocks a system?

FIGURE 2.1
Do you see this pile of rocks as a system?

Remember that a formal system contains components, interdependence, and aim.

- **Components:** There are many rocks in this pile, so it contains plenty of components.
- **Interdependence:** Aside from gravity, friction, and location, there is not much that links the rocks together.
- **Aim:** The rocks have a great deal of potential and could be used in many different ways, but in their current state they do not have a purpose.

Now consider Figure 2.2. Does the bridge depict a formal system?

Again, a formal system contains components, interdependence, and aim.

- **Components:** The bridge is made up of rocks and mortar.
- **Interdependence:** There are many connections between the rocks. Cement and mortar hold the rocks in their stacked and organized form. Capstones protect the connections from the weather. The connections are secure and close. The interdependence of these rocks creates a useful bridge.

FIGURE 2.2
Do you see this rock bridge as a system?

- **Aim:** The aim of these rocks is evident. They will safely transport people and vehicles using the structure that spans the river.

The pile of rocks may fit a loose, general definition of an informal system. But when applying the definition of a formal system, the pile of rocks does not qualify. The bridge, on the other hand, with its interdependence, components, and aim, is a formal system. In the same way, a bunch of tools is not a formal system, neither is a bunch of processes, even if the tools or processes live under the same roof. Geographic location does not create a formal system.

SYSTEMS DRIVE BEHAVIOR

In an organization, systems will develop—on purpose or haphazardly—to get the work done. All systems create the conditions that cause people to behave in a specific way. Successful organizations thoughtfully design their systems to produce a culture of sustainable excellence. Such systems foster and support the behavior of the individuals at work within them. A system that lacks design and purpose will evolve on its own and produce enormous variation.

Research done by the Shingo Institute indicates that if an organization has a clear purpose that the people support, then people will do the right thing to help accomplish that purpose—even if it is difficult. However, research also indicates that if the system is not changed to make it easy to do the right thing, then people will give up and revert to doing the wrong, easy thing.* The behavior driven by the system wins out in the long run.

THREE ESSENTIAL SYSTEMS

Of the myriad possible business systems, we are limiting our focus to three types of systems where the components are tightly connected: work systems, management systems, and the improvement system. These three broad categories of systems will give you a way to analyze and understand the specific systems in your organization, the people who work within them, the work they do, and how they are connected and interdependent.

The three essential organizational systems described in detail in this book will help you to think systemically about your organization.

THE SYSTEMS CONTRIBUTION

Designing systems is like following a recipe to make a nice omelet. When you gather and prepare the ingredients, it does not matter how perfectly you have chopped the vegetables or how nice your cheese or meat might be. If you leave the ingredients on the counter, you will never eat a nice meal. If you want to make an omelet, you must combine and cook the ingredients together. Making the effort to formalize the systems in your organization will ensure that everyone is working together to make the omelet.

---

* Troy Mumford, "Cultural Strata Effects: How Lean Culture Drivers of Engagement Vary by Employees' Level in the Organization" (speech, Shingo European Conference, Copenhagen, Denmark, December 2016).

One of the first steps of designing the systems of your organization is to create a controlled vocabulary. Defining language so that each person at your organization knows what is meant by *system* and other important words will facilitate the communication required for interdependence. Controlling vocabulary is also a way to create and support the culture of excellence. You will be best served to create your own system glossary with the people in your organization. The work of clear communication requires everyone to agree on which words should be in the glossary and what those words mean.

One of the *Three Insights of Organizational Excellence* states that "purpose and systems drive behavior."* The connection between systems and behaviors is an important foundation for the concepts in this book. System behaviors will be shown as follows.

> **KEY BEHAVIORAL INDICATOR: CLEAR COMMUNICATION**
> Control vocabulary by creating a system glossary.
> Identify systems that need to be designed.

To fully reap the benefits of this methodology, the definition of *system* must become part of the organization's language. Everyone must understand how they fit into a system—as both a contributor and a recipient.

The *Shingo Model* also teaches that

> all work in organizations is the outcome of a system. Systems must be designed to produce a specific end goal, otherwise they evolve on their own. Systems create the conditions that cause people to behave in a certain way. One of the outcomes of poorly designed systems is enormous variation in behavior or even consistently bad behavior.†

In many organizations work is done in informal, unstructured, undocumented systems. The systems lack clarity, which leaves the members of these systems in the fog. An informal system seldom includes formal

---

* Shingo Institute, *The Shingo Model*, 10.
† Shingo Institute, *The Shingo Model*, 15.

Informal Actions and Formal Systems		
Activity	**Informal Actions**	**Formal Systems**
Tire Change	On the side of the road	NASCAR pit crew
Travel	Hitchhiking	Japanese trains
Navigation	Verbal directions (pass the big tree, turn left)	GPS directions (google maps, Garmin, etc.)
Landscaping	Weed patch	Manicured garden
Maintenance	Fix when broken	Preventative maintenance
Planning	Make it up as we go	Strategic plan

TABLE 2.2

Note the huge gap between informal actions and formal systems. Work can happen through informal actions, but it is not as effective as work facilitated by a formalized system

system planning. Informal systems make it difficult for people to do the right thing even when they are giving their best efforts. Focusing on the three essential system types will guide you through the process of identifying your existing informal systems, help you find the parts that may be missing, and provide a framework for connecting components into functioning formal systems. Deming taught, "It is not enough to do your best; you must know what to do, and then do your best."* When a person reaches the limit of their understanding, they will stop, hesitate, or make things up.

Consider the activities in Table 2.2. Activities such as landscaping and maintenance can be accomplished through informal actions or formal systems. However, the activities within a formal system will be completed with higher quality and less waste.

The effort to design the systems of your organization by moving from general to specific, from informal to formal, and from undocumented to documented will create a sustainable culture of excellence.

KEY BEHAVIORAL INDICATOR: DOCUMENT YOUR SYSTEMS

We document the systems in order to provide connection, collaboration, communication, and consistency. Chapters 5, 6, and 7 provide details for how to document your systems.

---

* The W. Edwards Deming Institute, "Quotes by W. Edwards Deming," accessed April 15, 2020, https://quotes.deming.org/authors/W._Edwards_Deming/quote/10084.

3

Three Essential Systems

SYSTEMS DESIGN

What does it mean to design a system? Systems design is the action of defining the components of existing and new systems and implementing the five tools for each system. Once components are identified and tools are implemented, the system is formalized. In designing each system, you will identify all of the vital parts and organize them into the system. Designing a system can be a bit like cooking; not only do you need the right ingredients; you also need to use the ingredients in the right proportion at the right time.

Previously, many people who followed the Shingo Institute's recipe for excellence found it difficult to distinguish between tools and systems. Making a clear distinction between the two is very helpful. Think of the system as the recipe and the tools as the ingredients. Companies have many tools. Considering ingredients in the pantry is like looking at all the different tools. When the tools are combined together in the right way—as a system—you will get the dish that you want.

Implementing carefully considered, well-designed systems create and drive improvement throughout an organization by ensuring that each team member understands the work and is granted permission to do that work. Despite wanting to do their best, people can only do what they understand, and they will only do what they have permission to do. A formalized system gives workers the permission and the knowledge to make correct decisions about their work. The more closely the system functions to identify, support, and encourage the ideal behavior, the more sustainable the system becomes. The goal of any system should be to make it easy for people to do the right thing (the ideal behavior) and hard for people to do the wrong thing (the less-than-ideal behavior). Formalized systems create culture and drive behaviors.

DOI: 10.4324/9781003267768-3

THREE TYPES OF SYSTEMS

Many organizations struggle with what happens when a supervisor is not available to solve a problem. Oftentimes the work stops until the supervisor arrives, or each team member improvises a solution that creates as many unique workarounds as there are workers. Both responses are problematic. A well-designed system empowers each team member to make and respond correctly to problems as they arise. Because different team members are faced with different types of problems, they require different institutional support. The kind of system required to support each team member can be classified into the three types of systems identified by the Shingo Institute: management systems, work systems, and the improvement system.

While the exact dynamics of these types of systems will be unique to each organization, understanding the types of systems and how they relate to each other will help you to strengthen connections and empower people throughout your organization. Because the formalized systems provide the required information, team members are empowered to make decisions, find improvements, conduct audits, hold training, and report problems. A well-designed system also aligns all team members with the organization's purpose.

In Figure 3.1, notice that the management and improvement systems both point to the work system. This is because both systems support the

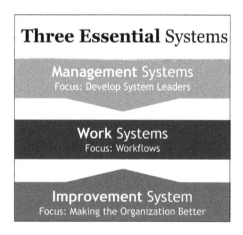

FIGURE 3.1

In an organization, the work systems are central. The improvement system and management systems contribute to the success of the work systems.

work of the organization. Of the three types of systems, the work system is the most fundamental. A work system has an internal focus, meaning that it focuses on everything that is needed for an output, i.e., the work being done to provide value to the customer.

The improvement system focuses *across* the entire organization and through all the departments within the organization. In this way, the systems support building an improvement culture that involves everyone in the organization, everywhere in the organization, all the time.

The focus of the management system is leading the organization by developing system leaders. The purpose of management systems should be to build alignment in the organization around the common purpose and to create value for the customers. However, these purposes are accomplished by the work systems, as supported by the improvement system. Through developing system leaders, the management system assures the work is done, and that continuous improvement is happening throughout the entire organization (Figure 3.2).

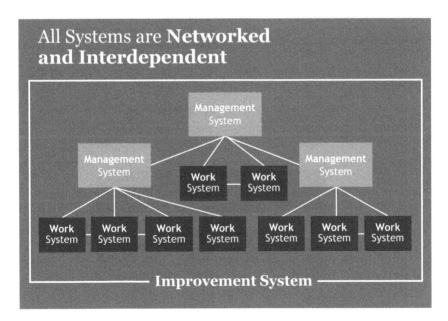

FIGURE 3.2
When formalized, all three types of systems work together to improve the organization.

The three types of systems are tightly connected and interdependent. Each type of system is dependent on the others. When the systems work together, the whole organization aims at excellence together.

WORK SYSTEMS

The work system is the basic organizational unit in the company and is usually the easiest of the three types to recognize (Figure 3.3). A work system consists of workflows or jobs. In an accounting work system, the people who are doing the same job would make up a workflow. For example, accounts receivable would be one workflow and accounts payable would be another. In manufacturing, a work system is often defined by product line. The process to manufacture the product is often arranged into cells and a work system could encompass multiple cells.

Because work systems are so fundamental, in most organizations they are functional units that can be found on an organizational chart. The leaders of work systems are generally supervisors or managers, easily identified on an existing organizational chart. While it is likely that you can identify some work systems in your company, they are most likely informal or lack some components of a formal system. A medium-size organization of a thousand people could have 20–40 work systems.

FIGURE 3.3
The work systems are central to the basic structure of the organization.

READER CHALLENGE

Identify a few of the work systems in your organization:

_____

_____

_____

The Real World: O.C. Tanner

O.C. Tanner is a global company that develops strategic employee recognition and reward solutions that help people accomplish and appreciate great work. They manufacture custom awards for recognizing the work people do from trophies to pins as well as apps to connect people to purpose, accomplishment, and to one another. O.C. Tanner received the Shingo Prize in 1999 and has continued to work closely with the Shingo Institute. They create "custom, one-of-a-kind products produced with the same efficiency as mass production."[*]

O.C. Tanner formalized these ten work systems:

- Distribution
- Purchasing
- International purchasing
- Logistics
- Maintenance
- Research and development
- Pressed product
- Custom product
- Build engineering
- Production scheduling/systems

The Real World: Toyota

Toyota gives us a great example of the importance of clearly defining the work processes in a system.[†] Although many companies have tried to

---

[*] *Business Wire*, "O.C. Tanner Executive Inducted into AME Hall of Fame," November 16, 2015, https://www.businesswire.com/news/home/20151116006236/en/O.C.-Tanner-Executive-Inducted-AME-Hall-Fame.

[†] Steve Spear and H. Kent Bowen, "Decoding the DNA of the Toyota Production System," *Harvard Business Review*, Sept–Oct (1999): 98.

imitate Toyota, most of them fail. Unsuccessful adoptions frequently focus on the obvious practices without applying the four unwritten rules:

1. All work is highly specified in its content, sequence, timing, and outcome.
2. Each team member knows who provides what and when.
3. Every product and service flows along a simple specified path.
4. Any improvement to process, worker/machine connections, or flow path must be made through the scientific method, under a teacher's guidance, at the lowest possible organizational level.

Like strands of DNA, these rules govern how people carry out their jobs, how they interact with each other, how products and services flow, and how people identify and process problems.

Following the Toyota example of improving processes, system design takes a similar deliberate scientific approach to improving systems.

IMPROVEMENT SYSTEMS

The improvement system consists of several sub-systems that impact all of the other systems in an organization (Figure 3.4). Each sub-system can be considered a separate system and should be comprised of all the essential tools and components of a full system. When working together,

FIGURE 3.4
The improvement system impacts the whole organization.

these sub-systems support improving the whole organization. Therefore, we teach a singular improvement system.

The human body is a good analogy. The body itself is a system with essential sub-systems, such as cardiovascular, digestive, lymphatic, etc. The improvement system or an organization likewise contains many sub-systems.

The focus of the improvement system is on making the organization better by driving improvement across all systems. As the sub-systems advance in development, the common focus of the different sub-systems will merge into the overarching improvement system. Common improvement sub-systems include problem-solving, 5S, SMED, visual management, and idea generation and tracking. The leaders of the improvement system and the various sub-systems are generally in the middle management tier of an organization. They are able to influence other leaders. A medium-size organization of a thousand people could have between 8 and 12 sub-systems to formalize within the improvement system.

READER CHALLENGE

What are the important improvement sub-systems at your organization?

_____

_____

_____

_____

_____

The Real World: O.C. Tanner

O.C. Tanner has formalized these improvement sub-systems*:

- Coaching and training
- Visual management

---

* To listen to Gary Peterson of O.C. Tanner talk about these functions, use the YouTube link: https://youtu.be/uzkFH5ISLKY. The video, "O.C. Tanner Lean Manufacturing Principles," was published by O.C. Tanner in 2014.

- Go and observe
- Problem-solving
- Leader daily work

MANAGEMENT SYSTEMS

Management systems consist of work systems and the improvement system (Figure 3.5). As explained above, its focus is the development of system leaders. A management system provides direction to the leaders of work systems and the improvement system. The management system would be led by an executive or top manager of the organization. The management system leaders ensure that the interrelationships between the work systems are properly developed and that the improvement system functions are adopted throughout the organization. Examples of management systems in a traditional organization might be operations, finance, HR, supply, strategy deployment, business development, customer relations, and R&D. Some organizations have moved all of these functions into a value stream organizational structure. Management systems may also have work systems that are the responsibility of the management system leader, such as business development. A medium-size organization of a thousand people could have between six and ten management systems.

FIGURE 3.5
The management system develops leaders for all types of systems.

READER CHALLENGE

What management systems can you list for your organization?

_____

_____

_____

_____

The Real World: Lifetime Products

As a pioneer of the System Design approach, Lifetime Products has been identifying and working with systems for nearly ten years. They have 16 functioning management systems:

- Manufacturing process
- Metals
- Plastics
- Manufacturing engineering
- Maintenance
- Product development
- Information technology
- Legal
- Planning/control
- Purchasing
- Quality
- Logistics
- Sales
- Marketing
- Human resources
- Accounting

As we have narrowed our focus to the three essential types of systems that will support striving for excellence, the hundreds of potential systems become more manageable. How many systems are we talking about? For most mature, medium-size organizations, we would expect about 50 systems (e.g., 32 work systems, 10 improvement sub-systems, and 8 management systems). Fifty well-defined, carefully thought out, formalized systems will be more helpful in aiming for excellence than hundreds of undefined, informal systems.

Your work as a systems designer will be to identify the specific systems in your organization and to formalize them by implementing the five required communication tools: standard work, reports, feedback, schedules, and improvement log, as well as other essential components such as a specified leader, and a clear aim.

While the systems in your organization may not add up perfectly to 50, you will be able to count and chart each system.

KEY BEHAVIORAL INDICATOR: DOCUMENT YOUR SYSTEMS

Identify each system
Chart each system

READER CHALLENGE

What is the first management system you would want to formalize in your organization?

_____

What are the two improvement sub-systems that you would want to formalize first?

_____

What are the three or four work systems you would want to formalize first?

_____

_____

_____

4

Five Required Tools

The true potential of implementing systems that drive behavior comes from defining the system components (or formalizing communication). The five required communication tools—standard work, reports, feedback, schedules, and improvement log—are the key components to designing and implementing systems.

The Shingo Institute discusses Shigeo Shingo's concept of tools in this way:

> *Shingo described the concept of a tool as a technique for solving a specific problem, necessary but not sufficient by itself to solve broader problems. Tools should be selected to enable a system to perform its intended purpose. Think of a system as a collection of tools working together to accomplish an intended outcome.**

In the system design approach presented in this book, we narrow the focus to five essential tools.

Every system is made up of physical components, such as equipment, raw material, documents, finished goods, even the facility or space. The five required tools connect all of the physical components together in order to accomplish the aim of the system. Regardless of the exact make-up of the components of a particular system, the five required tools establish and strengthen the connections among the components. The following discussion of each tool will help you to understand what we mean and begin to appreciate the value that each tool provides. (While we have numbered the tools here for ease of reading, there is no hierarchical significance to the numbering. Each tool is valuable and all are meant to work together.)

---

* Shingo Institute, *The Shingo Model*, 38.

DOI: 10.4324/9781003267768-4

TOOL #1: STANDARD WORK

Standard work is written documentation of the best current way to complete a specific process. Each process and operation requires a living document that captures the current best way to complete the work. This standard work provides the foundation for training, process validation, and improvement. An example of standard work is the list of steps for correctly, precisely, and efficiently operating equipment. Many organizations already have standard work in operation areas. Fewer organizations have standard work established for support areas. As you begin to formalize systems at your organization, you will need to assess the current state of existing standard work, and you may need to create additional standard work.

Adhering to standard work increases consistency in the work and the stability of output. Workers can only perform to the best of their knowledge and understanding. If each team member (or shift) has a different understanding of what to do, variation in process and output will result. One of the main purposes of employing standard work is to reduce variation.

Standard work must not only be written down, it must also be accessible and validated. When team members can consult the standard work before needing to ask the supervisor, they are empowered to solve problems they encounter. Trusting team members in this manner shows respect and humility while also freeing supervisors from constantly firefighting. When consulting standard work to solve a problem, a team member can easily determine if the problem may have been caused by not following standard work. If standard work was not followed, then the next step in solving the problem is clear and easy: follow the documented steps. If the problem stems from something new or something outside of the existing standard work, after completing problem-solving steps, standard work may need to be updated to avoid similar problems in the future.

Using standard work to solve problems creates an opportunity for productive communication and focus on the process, rather than stressed-out finger pointing, when problems arise.

The Real World: Lifetime Products

Concerned that standard work was not being followed, Dave Winter, chief manufacturing officer for Lifetime Products, identified the following problems with standard work:

It had been written by someone outside of the process.

It had been written in fantasy format (i.e., what we'd *like* to do, not what we *are* doing).

It had been placed in three-ring binders that collected dust.

It had not been written at all.

To educate everyone on the importance of standard work, Winter came up with the following guidelines for standard work:

Capture Your Current State
- Document your crappy process.
- Don't get hung up on format.
- It has to work for you.
- It should be very easy to update and flexible.
- Follow your documented process exactly.
- Audit to ensure process execution.
- Identify gaps in the documented process once you are consistently following your standard work.
- Problems will be easily seen.
- This creates opportunity for improvement.
- Improve the problems.
- Make new mistakes.

KEY BEHAVIORAL INDICATORS: STANDARD WORK

Include standard work as the best current way in your organization's glossary.

Document your best current process.

Follow your documented process exactly.

Validate standard work to ensure process execution.

Capture variation as you validate standard work.

Problem solve to eliminate variation.

Update standard work as improvements are made.

The Real World: O.C. Tanner

The production workers at O.C. Tanner review their standard work constantly. Manufacturing process steps are assigned to an RFID cup that accompanies the raw materials for the item being created. Detailed standard work is accessible from a dedicated touch screen located at each operation or station on the line (LIDS: lean information delivery system). Detailed procedures may be text, but they also include pictures and videos of complicated portions of the process. Review of standard work can be done in real time.

TOOL #2: REPORTS

Information or data used to make decisions about or complete work is a part of the system communication tool called reports, a broad category of all data used in the system. Like standard work, reports must be accessible to team members. Reports must also present applicable data in a fit-for-use format. Of course, any data offered to team members must be relevant and accurate.

Data alone does not create a useful report. When designing a system, it is important to ensure that the data will be useful and necessary. In many organizations, data is either difficult for a team member to find and use or so plentiful that it is difficult to know which is the most important to use. For example, a call center team member is not likely to leave their desk, locate the key to a locked office, remember the password to the computer where the necessary data is kept, and then create a custom query to find data needed to make a decision. Difficult-to-use or acquire data will be ignored. Remember that a major reason for formalizing systems is to create a culture in which team members are authorized to make decisions about their work. In many cases, only the supervisor has access to the data. As you design the system, your goal is to provide each team member with the exact data he or she needs to make good decisions about the work.

The reports tool can take many different forms. A report may be printed or digital. It may be a standard set of data created by a database specialist or it may be a query created by an individual. It may be part of a dashboard displayed on a computer screen that a team member checks daily to identify assignments. It may be a regular email of quality control statistics. Data displayed on a communication board also counts as a report.

When designing a system, part of the design work is to ensure that the right data gets to the right person at the right time. The right person is the one who can use that data to make a decision. As you consider the myriad of data available, it may help you to focus by answering these questions: (1) what decision can be made from this data, and (2) who should make that decision?

Good reports funnel exactly the right data to exactly the right person at the time it is needed to make good decisions. For example, a report that the whole plant is on schedule today is not easy for team members in a specific manufacturing cell to apply. However, a report about whether or not their specific cell is on time or behind is data they can immediately use.

The Real World: Lifetime Products

A transportation work system at Lifetime Products uses these reports:

- Vehicle inspection logbook
- Department of Transportation (DOT) files
- Yard management system (internal shipping database)
- Kaizen form
- Safety (near-miss reports)
- Truck management database

Some of the transportation data is kept on clipboards, some of it is on communication boards, and much of the data is in an internal database. All of the data needed to operate the transportation work system, regardless of format, is part of the report tool.

KEY BEHAVIORAL INDICATORS: REPORTS

Ensure that the data is up to date.

Ensure that the report data is accurate.

Train team members to understand the data and the decisions to be made.

Ensure that all data is formatted for the use of the decision maker.

Ensure that each report is needed by the people who are intended to use it.

TOOL #3: FEEDBACK

Feedback is personal communication regarding the work. Feedback can be spoken or written but it always occurs between people. While a computer-generated report is communication, it is not personal feedback until it is reviewed and discussed by someone. For example, a form email regarding insurance enrollment is not personal feedback; however, a note sent from a supervisor in the form of a text, email, or letter is feedback. Feedback may take place as a discussion between people about a report or standard work. Most of the feedback is reviewing the four other tools. In this way, the five required communication tools facilitate conversation about the work and create tight connections throughout the system.

The following questions are good examples of how feedback can be initiated by a supervisor:

- Do you have any questions about the standard work?
- Are there steps in the standard work that are difficult to follow?
- Is there any of the data that is not helpful?
- Is there data that is difficult to use?

How often do team members receive personal feedback from supervisors, peers, customers, and others? In some organizations the answer could be seldom or never. In most organizations it's not often enough. Many supervisors find the idea of an annual review daunting and many team members find such a meeting nerve wracking. However, both supervisor and team member are more comfortable with regular discussions of the work.

The Real World: O.C. Tanner

At O.C. Tanner, production team members receive feedback from their huddle at the beginning of each shift. When the members of the work cell gather at the huddle board, they discuss safety, recognition, the work of the previous shift (quality, cost, and delivery), the targets for their shift, beginning workstation assignments, and daily rotation. They use reports on targets and quality to facilitate their discussion. Throughout the day, the leader is on the line working and speaking with the operators, providing feedback.

The Real World: Elementary School Teachers

Elementary school teachers are masters at providing feedback. They constantly look over the shoulder of the student pointing out what work is correct and ask questions to guide students to understand what is not correct or what needs more attention. Seldom does the teacher's specific and timely feedback cause hurt feelings in the students. Students expect correction. Teachers deliver correction about the work completed, but they are positive and encouraging about the intent and effort. Mistakes do not mean that a student is a failure; rather they help both the student and the teacher to learn.

TOOL #4: SCHEDULES

The schedule of feedback within a system is so crucial that it warrants its own spot among the five communication tools. There are many components of a system that require a schedule, but when we refer to the schedule tool, we specifically mean scheduling feedback. If feedback is not scheduled, it is our experience that it does not happen.

As you design each system, you will identify the frequency or cadence at which feedback is required. Often, regular feedback is built into every workday, such as a morning huddle. Other regular feedback might include a weekly meeting to review the measurements of the area. Some feedback might be scheduled based on a team member's time with the organization, such as a new employee receiving feedback every four hours for the first week. In a well-designed system, the supervisor spends a great deal of time giving individual feedback to the members of the team (Figure 4.1).

The Real World: Feedback at Lifetime
Products Transportation Work System

In the Transportation Work System at Lifetime Products, the schedule of feedback looks like this:

- Daily: vehicle inspection logbook
- Weekly: equipment inspection spot checks

Schedule of Feedback	
Daily	Daily huddle
Weekly	Go and Observe walk
Monthly	Performance review
Quarterly	System review
Annually	Strategic plan review

FIGURE 4.1
A possible supervisor's feedback schedule.

- Bi-weekly: Over the Road (OTR) load securement inspection
- Quarterly: 15 Hostler safety audits and review of each standard work process

KEY BEHAVIORAL INDICATORS: SCHEDULE

Determine feedback cadence of the system.
Schedule the feedback.
Adhere to the schedule.
Review the schedule for improvements.

Note: Scheduling each feedback session may be done by different people, such as a manager or supervisor, a team member, or the person receiving the feedback.

When it comes to feedback, we often have good intentions and weak follow-through. The scheduled feedback becomes an important part of leader standard work.

TOOL #5: IMPROVEMENT LOG

An improvement log is a document that captures improvement ideas and assignments. The improvement log is the anchor of a multi-step process:

- **Capture** all reasonable improvement opportunities
- **Evaluate** and prioritize the ideas
- **Assign** the selected improvement opportunity to the person best able to complete the assignment
- **Identify** and supply needed resources
- **Track** implementation

Capture

The first part of the improvement log process is noticing and listening carefully to improvement opportunities. It is important to capture in writing improvement ideas as they happen. Take note of opportunities immediately before the ideas fly away. Ideas generated during meetings or feedback sessions or reviews should be captured by a scribe. At this point, all reasonable ideas should be noted, although there is no expectation that they will all be used. It is important to keep all reasonable ideas because ideas multiply by inspiring other ideas. Perhaps the sixth idea is the breakthrough idea, but you wouldn't get there without the previous ideas.

Evaluate

When capturing ideas, you want to capture all of them in the notes, but that will create too many potential actions. You must create a way to evaluate and prioritize the ideas in your notes that will make it into the log. There should be a scheduled discussion of potential assignments for improvement. It may be tempting to skip or short-change the step of evaluating and prioritizing ideas, but there is little point in assigning an improvement task if it is not concrete, immediately applicable, and worthy of resources to implement. There needs to be a correct balance of the number of ideas that make it into the improvement log. Too many ideas will overwhelm the available resources. Too few ideas in the improvement log means that opportunities will be missed. Some improvement ideas need to be referred to someone outside your area. Some improvement ideas, such as a safety idea, need to be quickly escalated in the organization.

Make Assignments

The improvement log becomes the place where the discussion of improvement opportunities becomes formalized by making an assignment. How do you know how many improvement ideas should be implemented? You should assign as many good ideas as you have resources to complete. Usually, there will be between three and five active assignments on the log. As an assignment is completed, additional assignments can be placed on the log.

How many improvement logs are there in an organization? There should be an improvement log for each system. At the beginning of the book, we discussed that some organizations identified so many systems that it was unhelpful. The same could happen with improvement logs. Once the work systems, improvement system, and management systems are clearly defined, an improvement log per system is reasonable because improvements logged are specific to the system.

Identify and Supply Resources

Once the improvement idea is assigned to the right person, that person will need appropriate resources to research the improvement proposed, experiment with countermeasures, implement the best one, and ensure that it sustains. Resources may simply be time and permission to work out the implementation details. Listing assignments in the improvement log can help to facilitate the discussion about needed resources.

Track

Because the improvement log contains all the details of improvement assignments, it is also used to track the progress. When an idea is entered into the improvement log and assigned, it is given a due date. Reviewing the due date of an assignment is a good way of evaluating the progress. The log also serves as a record of all the improvements completed and supports accountability.

READER CHALLENGE

How are you doing? Note how your organization currently employs an improvement log in each system.

Capture improvement ideas: _____

Evaluate and prioritize improvement ideas: _____

Assign resources: _____

Track implementation: _____

The Real World: O.C. Tanner

In the Delivery Work System at O.C. Tanner, some items recorded in the improvement log of the spring of 2020 include:

- How can we best measure UK on time? (Orders can be late from US teams.)
- Need to get drop ships working
- Next steps to eliminate Delivery status report

KEY BEHAVIORAL INDICATORS: IMPROVEMENT LOG

Ensure that a scribe is assigned to capture ideas at key meetings or reviews.
Schedule evaluation and prioritization of improvement ideas.
Ensure that the improvement log is up to date.

Note: The system leader owns the system map and therefore is responsible for all components. In some cases, a system leader is very interested in the outcomes from the improvement log but is not interested in administering the details of the improvement log. The way to resolve this conflict is to simply assign the improvement log upkeep to a system member. This can be a good opportunity to provide experience to future leaders.

Other Essential Components

Every system also requires four other essential components: a leader, an aim, a scope, and system team members. The focus of the system leader is to ensure that the people and tools are functioning properly to accomplish the aim of the system. A system without a clearly defined leader supporting it will fail because adherence to the system will break down.

The aim of a system should explain *why* the system exists and how the system fits into the overall purpose of the organization. The system scope varies by type of system, and it will be explored more thoroughly in the following chapters. The system team members should be those who work within the system, but it does not include customers. For example, an accounting work system in some organizations will include accounts payable, accounts receivable, and collections, among others, but team members do not include everyone who receives a paycheck from accounts payable.

The Why of Systems

The process of formalizing systems by defining and employing all components, including the five communication tools, is the way to design and maintain stable systems. The constant need to respond to problems stems from an organizational culture where systems are informal and supervisors hold all of the knowledge and power. In such a culture, the supervisor must direct every bit of work and respond to every problem. This leaves a supervisor no time to plan, direct, encourage, teach, or recognize the work. Supervisors need to spend time developing systems rather than just reacting or responding to problems. Systems need to be deliberately designed. Implementing and documenting the five communication tools and the other essential components is what we mean by designing and formalizing a system.

Systems need to be deliberately designed. Implementing and documenting the five communication tools and the other essential components is what we mean by designing and formalizing a system.

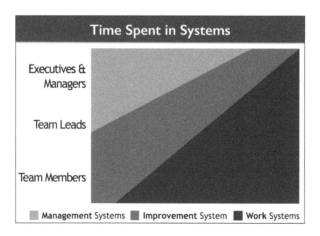

TABLE 4.1

Leaders at different organizational levels will spend their time differently as they work on systems

Formalized systems provide team members the information they need to solve problems more effectively and efficiently. The communication tools can aid problem-solving efforts. When a problem arises, consider the following questions:

- **Standard work:** Was the standard work followed? Does the standard work need to be updated?
- **Reports:** Was the needed data available, useable, and accurate?
- **Feedback:** Has a personal relationship been created so that the team member is comfortable reporting and solving the problem?
- **Schedule:** Has the cadence of the feedback been understood and consistently followed?
- **Improvement log:** Is there an existing idea to solve the problem? Has the idea been given sufficient resources and time to correct the problem?

As you formalize systems at your organization, the amount of time workers spend with each of the three types of systems will vary. Team members will spend nearly all of their time within the work systems with a little bit of time spent with the improvement system. Team leads will spend about half their time with the work systems and improvement system with a little bit of time spent with the management systems. Managers and executives will spend the most time with management systems (Table 4.1).

Formalized systems can consist of many components. At a minimum, a formalized system must include (1) the five required communication tools, (2) a name, (3) an assigned leader, (4) a clear aim, (5) boundaries defined by workflow/jobs and team members, and (6) identified interconnectivity with improvement and management systems. The five communication tools are required because they create stable systems by building strong connections and effective communication within and between systems.

5

What Do We Mean by System Design?

An architect designs a building by creating a blueprint (Figure 5.1). An engineer designs a new part by creating a schematic drawing. A tailor designs a suit by creating a pattern. There are many different facets of design, but all designers use a standard method to succinctly communicate the details of their designs. As you take on the role of systems designer, you will need to be able to capture and organize all the components of the system in a document.

The Shingo Institute has chosen a system "map" as the format to be used by system designers. The system map is the final product of your design work. When the system map is completed, you will have formalized the system. Not only is the map itself the evidence of a formalized system, but completing the map will guide you through the system design process. It then becomes a living document through which the system can be reviewed and improved upon (Figure 5.2).

Since improvement is a journey, we call our document a map. A map is a visual representation of geography. It includes roads, rivers, lakes, points of interest, and natural features. Similarly, a system map is a visual representation of a system. A system map includes the five required communication tools (standard work, reports, schedule, feedback, and improvement log), two results (KPI and KBI), and other needed components, such as system name, system leader, system aim, and system members.

System maps are used for the following purposes:

- Identifying the components of a system.
- Organizing the components with focus on the five required communication tools.
- Identifying system members.

DOI: 10.4324/9781003267768-5

- Assessing (or comparing what you're doing to what's on the map).
- Identifying, capturing, and assigning improvements in the improvement log.
- Training new leaders and team members when a change occurs.

FIGURE 5.1
A blueprint captures the design of a building.

FIGURE 5.2
A map simplifies geography, making it possible to plan a road trip.

The next three chapters will guide you through completing a system map for each of the three essential systems: work, improvement, and management. As each type of system has its unique focus and structure, each has its own specific map as well. Example maps are shown in Chapters 6, 7, and 8 (Figure 5.3).

As we present the system maps, we will give specific details. The maps are provided as templates or examples to help your organization strengthen the current state of its systems. They are not intended to be prescriptions. We don't expect you to do exactly what is shown on the example maps. We know that you will compare the details to

FIGURE 5.3
System maps capture and simplify the complexity of an organization's relationships.

your own situation. We invite you to modify and adapt the examples. Keep what makes sense and adapt or change the rest to work in your organization. That said, we also advise caution as you adapt. There is a purpose for each component included and a reason we require the five communication tools. Along with Deming, we define a system as "a *network of interdependent components.*" When a component is removed, it changes how the system works.

In the following chapters, you will also see examples of completed maps of a work system, improvement system, and management system. It is unlikely that any organization would complete all three different types of maps for the entire organization at once. The development of systems happens organically—it will start in one section and then expand—and it takes time. Of course, an organization that can adopt and implement system maps universally will reap the benefits of a systems approach to improvement sooner.

The beauty and magic of system maps is that they are able to work equally well in very diverse areas. Formalizing systems by using the Shingo system maps improves system stability, connections, collaboration, communication, and supports consistency.

As you begin to design systems you will start with what you have, your current state, which is a combination of programs, tools, processes, and measurements. Your design work will give them a common structure of components, including five system communication tools and two key outcomes. A formally designed system also has the following components:

1. Leader
2. Aim: The purpose of the system, the reason why the system exists, and how the system fits into the overall organization
3. Clear scope: A work system's scope is defined by workflows or jobs. The improvement system's scope is the entire organization. A management system's scope is defined by the work systems and improvement sub-systems that report to a leader
4. Members

We've presented the system map as a suggested format. The Shingo system map is in an Excel spreadsheet format. Some people may be more comfortable using a Word format. Any format could be used as long as the system is documented. For the system members to be on the same page, a page must exist. The details in the document will lead to the conversations that need to happen.

6

Work Systems

You will begin your work as a system designer with work systems (Figure 6.1). Of all the types of systems, the work system exists in the greatest number in an organization and is the easiest to understand. Work systems can often be found on an organizational chart because they are functional units like shipping, production, and accounting. Although you may be able to identify work systems in your organization, they are most likely lacking some components of a formal system. The Shingo Institute's work system map is a way to formalize the work systems in your organization.

WORK SYSTEM MAP

The work system map is the tool provided by the Shingo Institute to define the system components and to spark the discussions necessary to move from informal, casual systems to formal, stable systems. As you complete work system maps, you will need to get specific in defining each system. It is important to realize that you are capturing the current state on the work system map. The map is used in two different ways. As you first complete the map, it will assist you in formalizing the system. Once the map is completed, it will be the method of reviewing, tracking, and improving the performance of the system.

As you consider your own organization, you will find that informal systems already exist. You don't need to reorganize everything to implement systems thinking. Rather, you will work to formalize what exists in a system by defining all of the components, including the five

DOI: 10.4324/9781003267768-6

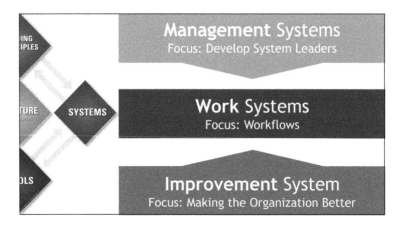

FIGURE 6.1
The Systems diamond of the *Shingo Model* has three types of systems.

required communication tools, and ensuring that they are being used consistently. Consider the example in Figure 6.2 of a work system map in the format recommended by the Shingo Institute.

Note that the color coding on the map matches the colors of the *Shingo Model*: Systems is green, Tools is red, Results is gold, and Culture is purple. You may note that there is no blue color for Principles on the maps. Principles are woven into every aspect of the map.

SYSTEMS

As you work through the map you will begin with the systems scope components in the upper left corner. The green-colored system information includes the system name, people involved (leader and team members), the aim, and workflows. These details define the boundaries of the system by listing what is included in the system.

Work System and Work System Leader

The system name in the top left allows for quick identification of the map. The leader is listed by name, while other team members can either be listed by name or position. In the example above, the system is named Shipping. Amy is the leader, and her team members are listed by position.

Work System Map

Work System	Work System Leader		Feedback	Frequency	wk1	wk2	wk3	wk4	wk5	wk6	wk7	wk8	wk9	wk10	wk11	wk12	wk13
Shipping	Amy	Aim	Shift Huddle	Daily	D	D	D	D	D	D	D	D	D	D	D	D	D
Aim			Leads Review	Daily	D	D	D	D	D	D	D	D	D	D	D	D	D
Ship finished goods safely, on-time, and without errors or damage. Engage everyone in continuous improvement.			Staff Meeting	Weekly	X	X	X	X	X	X	X	X	X	X	X	X	X
			Go & Observe Walk	Bi-Weekly		X		X		X		X	X			X	
Workflows			Review Imp. Log	Bi-Weekly	X	X		X		X	X	X	X			X	
Full truckload, less than truckload, parcel, export			Review Measurements	Monthly			X				X				X	X	
Team Members			Review WS Map	Quarterly							X						
Shippers, receivers, loaders, dispatch, inventory specialists																	

Standard Work	Reports	Imp. Sub-Systems
Truck Load Work Inst.	Shift Report	Idea Generation
LTL Work Inst.	Quality Report	Training
Parcel Work Inst.	Accident Reports	5S
International Work Inst.	Forms	Visual Management
Online Shipments	Orders	Problem Solving
	Database Queries	Voice of the Customer
	Display Boards	Safety

Work System Improvement Log

	Assign	Due	Status
5S project for Building H-1	George	28-Oct	50%
Audit work instructions for online shipments	Susan	11-Nov	35%
Create training materials for new shipping hires	Frank	14-Oct	100%
Research shipping damage on export orders	Juan	14-Oct	85%

Key Performance Indicators

	Goal	July	Aug	Sept
Ship on-time	95%	94%	96%	90%
Quality correct shipments to customer	99%	97%	98%	96%
Quality ship without product damage	99%	96%	94%	95%
Safety hours between accidents	10K	9.7K	15K	20K
Idea generation (1 per month per employee)	42	40	55	38

Key Behavioral Indicators

	KBI Status
Ensure reasonable and accurate ship-on-time target date	red
Standard work for account routing is followed	green
Standard work for shipping is followed and validated	green
Near misses are reported and resolved	yellow
Ideas are documented as they occur	yellow

FIGURE 6.2

This sample work system map shows the details of a shipping system.

Aim

Remember our definition of a system: "A system is a network of interdependent components that work together to try to accomplish the aim of the system. The aim of the system must be clear to everyone in the system."*

It may be helpful to think of the aim as a general statement of direction for the system. In this example, the aim of the shipping system is twofold: (1) ship finished goods safely, on time, and without errors or damage, and (2) engage everyone in continuous improvement.

Workflows

We need to distinguish between a work system and a workflow. At Lifetime Products metal is received into a fabrication work system. Everything that is needed to be done before the metal is powder coated is part of fabrication. The different operations within fabrication are punching, cutting, bending, and welding. These are the four workflows or jobs within the fabrication work system.

Which workflows belong in a system is determined by the way the work system is defined. A work system is generally determined by the number of people who can be led by one supervisor, manager, or team leader. In a very complex area of the business, there will be fewer people in the system. In simpler areas where many people do essentially the same job, the team can be larger. In most organizations, the existing organizational chart will match the major functions of the organizations. Begin with your existing organizational chart with an understanding that all of the people who are working together for a common output are part of a system. A work system is generally between 10 and 30 people.

Once a work system is identified based on the team that one person can supervise, the jobs or workflows within that system are generally easy to identify. Note the work system, workflow, and team members in the three examples of work systems in Table 6.1.

Olive Lewis can supervise ten people because nearly everyone is doing the same thing, working on the same type of equipment. In an

---

* Deming, *The New Economics*, 50. Emphasis added.

Work Systems Consistent with Organization Size			
	Small	**Medium**	**Large**
Work System	Finance	Accounting	Accounts Receivable
Work Flows and People	Finance reports: 1 Bookkeeping: 1	Accounts payable: 2 Accounts receivable: 3	Big box accounts: 3 Sporting goods: 2 Warehouse clubs: 2 Online accounts: 2 Int'l accounts: 1
Total Team Members	2	5	10
Supervisor	Megan Jones	Nancy Katz	Olive Lewis

TABLE 6.1

Organizations of different sizes will identify work systems consistent with their sizes

organization that has three shifts, there is still only one work system. The three supervisors work together to implement the five tools the same way across all shifts.

The reason it is necessary to identify workflows is that standard work, reports, and training are organized by workflow. You may ask, for example, what is the standard work for this workflow? What data or reports are necessary to complete the work? What is the necessary training for people in this job or workflow? Carefully identifying the workflows of a work system helps a leader assign people to jobs they are capable of and trained to do, thus allowing them to do their best work.

> **Carefully identifying the workflows of a work system helps a leader assign people to jobs they are capable of and trained to do, thus allowing them to do their best work.**

In the example map of the shipping system, the workflows are full truck load, less than a truck load, parcel, and export. Even though much of the work within the shipping system is similar, these four areas differ enough that the operators receive different training, use different warehouse locations, and use different materials, such as labels and carriers.

> **KEY BEHAVIORAL INDICATOR: WORKFLOWS**
>
> Build training on carefully identified workflows.

Team Members

A system, as defined by the Shingo Institute, includes the people who work together toward a common aim using the five communication tools and having KPIs and KBIs as measured outcomes. If the system includes a limited number of people, list them by name. If the system includes many people, list them by position.

Some systems interact a great deal with the rest of the company, e.g., IT and HR. Workers who receive payroll from HR or software training from IT do not belong to the IT or HR system; instead they are customers of the system. Some systems that impact the whole organization will have only a few people as team members.

In the sample system map shown above, the positions included are shippers (who send the product out), receivers (who get the product from the manufacturing line), dispatchers (who coordinate truck arrival and departure), and inventory specialists.

Improvement Sub-systems

The last component in the green system scope section of the map is the improvement sub-systems. Only list the improvement sub-systems that are applicable to your work system. Each of the organization's improvement sub-systems will be carefully detailed as its own system on its own improvement sub-system map. Including the applicable improvement sub-systems on the work system map is one way to recognize that the execution of the improvement sub-systems happens in the work system. Listing improvement sub-systems also strengthens connections between systems and the interdependence of the systems.

TOOLS

The *red* sections of the map are for the five required communication tools: standard work, reports, feedback, schedule, and improvement log.

Standard Work

The first tool to define on the system map is the standard work, the documented sequences of the best current way to complete processes and operations. The example map from the shipping department lists truck load work instructions, LTL work instructions, parcel work instructions, international work instructions, and online shipments.

Notice that these are categories of standard work. The work system map does not need to list individual processes or document names. This section of the map is not an index of all standard work; it is a place to list the organizational categories of standard work that pertain to the system.

Reports

While standard work relates to the processes of how work flows through the system, the reports relate to the information that flows through the system. System reports include all of the data that is used in the system. Reports capture and format the data necessary to do the work, including sales, customers, products, or services.

As you carefully consider the reports required in the system, it may help to realize that data can generally be categorized by how it is created or stored.

- Data entered into a company-wide financial database. For example, a Customer Relationship Management (CRM) database that includes sales, customer service, marketing, and inventory data.
     Preprogrammed computer-generated reports
     Individual query—unique one-time request for data
- Information in a standardized form stored electronically that is not part of the company-wide financial database.
     Attendance report
     Accident report

Quality report

Shift report

- Data created by filling out a standardized form by hand. Even though the data is not entered into the computer, the form needs to be filled out correctly.

  Purchasing requisition

  Improvement idea card

  Leave request

- Data created for display to the whole area in a communication board.

  Area whiteboard—updated by hand hourly or daily

- Data collected while assessing behavior in an area.

  Assessment Forms (See examples and explanation from Lifetime Products in Chapter 9.)

Regardless of its method of creation, correct, timely, fit-for-use data is needed to make decisions. Completing the work system map is an opportunity to carefully evaluate currently used data and identify data that may be missing, difficult for system members to use, or even not needed.

In the example work system map, reports include shift report, quality report, accident reports, forms, orders, database queries, and display boards (which may include several reports). When completing your work system map, reports may be listed by their specific name or grouped into categories.

Feedback

Feedback occurs when someone communicates with the system team members to review the work of the system. This can happen one-on-one or in a group, virtually or in person. During the feedback process, the reviewer, system leaders, and team members review all other system components with a specific focus on system communication tools. For example, is the standard work up to date? being followed? assessed? The same questions are asked of the reports, schedule, and improvement log.

According to *Gallup Business Journal*,* the number one predictor of employee turnover is the relationship with the immediate manager.

---

* Jennifer Robison, "Turning Around Employee Turnover," *Gallup Business Journal*, May 8, 2008, https://news.gallup.com/businessjournal/106912/turning-around-your-turnover-problem.aspx.

Personal relationships are generally founded on common interests. In your organization, the workplace itself is that common interest. Often, supervisors underestimate how much team members are interested in the job they are doing. Personal feedback is an opportunity to build relationships through discussion focused on the work. Supervisors may ask:

- How is each tool doing?
- How can each tool be improved?
- How do you think we can work together to do the job better?

Focusing on the communication tools allows leaders and workers to have shared expectations of behavior and results. The communication tools, when they are properly employed, reinforce the behaviors necessary to stabilize, maintain, and improve the system. When leaders listen carefully to the team members' responses, opportunities for improvement are quickly identified and ideal behavior is reinforced and recognized, providing an incentive for it to continue.

Sometimes leaders are concerned that workers will take their feedback as criticism. The work system map gives leaders a tool that enables regular communication with team members and, when appropriately employed, removes the fear of personal criticism because the discussion is about the map and its components. People are comfortable talking about the tools they use to get the job done. (Have you ever heard golfers discuss clubs? Or racers talk engines?) Discussing tools is not taken as personal criticism because inquiring about the effectiveness of a tool does not imply that the worker has done something wrong. For example, a supervisor might ask, "Is this report up to date and easy to use?" In addition, this can more deeply embed ideal behaviors that are informed by the principles in the Cultural Enablers dimension of the *Shingo Model:* Respect Every Individual and Lead with Humility.

Regular personal interaction that focuses on the work builds relationships and aligns everyone toward the same goal. Once it is completed, the work system map is an effective guide for feedback discussions. If you conscientiously fill out the map and focus on the communication tools, people will soon feel like they can contribute to improving the system. Teaching leaders how to communicate with team members about the systems communication tools has enormous value in an organization. The system map is a key to that communication.

Some feedback occurs in a group, rather than one-to-one. For example, a staff huddle is a short daily meeting for everyone within the system. Another example of feedback in a group is the weekly staff meeting, which would include the manager or supervisor and the team lead. Managers, supervisors, and team leads can be frustrated by spending so much time in meetings that seem non-value-added; however, meetings that are guided by the maps as a type of agenda can be a value-added form of feedback because they are directly related to the work the attendees are engaged in.

Feedback isn't one way. Leaders need to be prepared to receive feedback from team members. A good rule of thumb is for leaders to listen twice as much as they talk—they have two ears and only one mouth. A simple way to do that is to assign various team members to review data in a meeting, rather than having only the supervisor review the data.

You can see on the example work system map that feedback takes many forms: shift huddle, leads review, staff meeting, Go & Observe walk, review improvement log, review measurements, and review work system map.

Schedule/Cadence

The schedule section on the work system map refers specifically to the schedule of feedback. You can see from the example that each type of feedback is assigned a frequency. Once created, the work system map functions both as a schedule for the regular review of the system and as a mechanism for following up. The schedule/cadence section of the system map can be used to plot the desired intervals between feedback as shown in Figure 6.2. Ds (daily action) and Xs (indicates the scheduled time) or dates can be entered to schedule the time to meet.

To function properly, the work system map should be formally reviewed at the conclusion of each quarter. As the schedule is reviewed, simply highlight the meetings that occurred. This is a very simple and visual way to see how the schedule failed or succeeded. If a pattern of missing feedback opportunities occurs, it will need to be adjusted.

Improvement Log

The improvement log is the place to record improvement opportunities and assignments for the system. One important outcome of regular feedback is the opportunity to collect improvement ideas. Once those ideas have been prioritized and assigned for implementation, they are listed on the work system map. Improvement ideas entered into the log include a person to whom the task is assigned and a date the work is to be completed. The definition of an assignment is that it will require someone at least two hours to complete. Any improvement activity that takes less than two hours is considered a task, and tasks are not recorded on the system log. Only improvement assignments that will take place in the next three months are entered in the improvement log. The improvement log is not a wish list. It is a log of actual improvement activity that will be implemented.

In the sample work system map, the shipping department is pursuing four improvement ideas. Each assignment is due in October or November. When the work system map is reviewed, George, Susan, Frank, and Juan will each be ready to explain the progress they have made on their improvement assignments.

RESULTS: KEY PERFORMANCE INDICATORS

The results section of the map is colored gold. It contains the key performance indicators (KPI). This is the place on the work system map for performance metrics. A work system map should not have more than ten total measurements. The performance measures listed on the work system map must be for the specific work system and they must align to the organization or division KPIs.

In many organizations, KPIs are organized in a balanced scorecard and include quality, safety, delivery, cost, and morale. If these scorecards exist, it is acceptable to align the results section of the work system map to the existing scorecard. It is not necessary to create two scorecards.

For our shipping example, the key performance indicators are ship on time, correct shipments to customer, ship without product damage, safety hours between accidents, and idea generation. You may remember that a similar language was used for the aim of the system. The aim does not include metrics. In the key performance indicators section, the measurement and the formula to get that measurement should be defined and understood by everyone. Measurements should be up to date and used to make good decisions about the work of the system.

CULTURE: KEY BEHAVIORAL INDICATORS

The key behavioral indicators (KBIs) are colored purple for culture because they encapsulate the direction in which the culture needs to shift—always moving behavior closer to the ideal. KBIs are the carefully selected behaviors that will lead to the desired system performance results. (KBIs are frequently called leading indicators because close attention to the way the behaviors are practiced—what people actually do—can predict trends that show up later in KPI measurements.) As the system map is intended to be a living document, you should not be surprised to find your KBIs evolving. The first KBI chosen may not end up being the best, but it is a start. As the system improves and behavior matures, a better KBI may be discovered.

As an example, consider a sales organization measuring KPI in sales dollars. The most obvious KBI is the number of sales calls made. However, experience may show that a better indicator is the number of sales calls made to purchasing decision makers. Further refinement will focus on making calls to qualified purchasing decision makers. While the first insight from the *Shingo Model* tells us "ideal results require ideal behavior," it is unusual to find the ideal behavior on the first try.

Consider the relationship between KBIs and KPIs from the shipping system in this chapter's example map:

- "Ensure reasonable and accurate ship-on-time target date" will lead to the "ship on-time" key performance indicator.
- "Standard work for account routing is followed" will lead to "quality correct shipment to customer."
- "Following and validating standard work for shipping" will lead to "quality shipping without damage to the product."
- "Taking time to document improvement ideas as they occur" will result in "ideas being captured."

An important perspective on the KBI is that each action is performed by an individual. The improvement will happen because individual workers practice the actions that cumulatively move the measurement or the KPI.

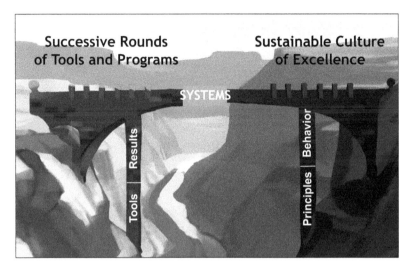

FIGURE 6.3
Formalized systems bridge the gap from successive rounds of programs to a sustainable culture of excellence.

When behaviors have been identified and broken down to the level of action, an individual can identify the action he or she can take that will improve the measurement. In this way, an individual can take ownership of the action. When individuals own and practice actions, they are empowered with the ability to change. And when the actions are practiced regularly and consistently, measurable change will follow.

SUMMARY

The work system map is the Shingo Institute's method of formalizing work systems and bridging the gap between successive rounds of programs and a sustainable culture of excellence based on principles (Figure 6.3). The work of creating a work system map formalizes the communication between people in the same system and creates a way to regularly review the work of the system. The work system map is crucial to create tight interdependencies among all of the components of a system.

7

Improvement System

The improvement system focuses on making the organization better so that its activity can affect the entire organization. The improvement system coordinates all of the improvement efforts across the organization through connections to each work system and management system. In many organizations, improvement efforts are often in the form of programs and are not an integrated part of the overall improvement system. As programs, improvement efforts often struggle to be sustained over time or to expand in scope to impact the entire organization. For example, when organizations deploy Lean teams or an improvement specialist, often their expertise fails to reach the whole organization. Initial program enthusiasm can be sustained by formalizing the improvement program into a sub-system of the overall improvement system, and then by connecting each sub-system to management and work systems. The people doing the work of improving are in the work systems. The management systems provide direction to the improvement sub-systems.

> **Masaaki Imai of the Kaizen Institute and a Shingo Academy member has said that continuous improvement is** *"everyday improvement, everybody improvement, and everywhere improvement."**

As you look at the programs through the lens of systems, you will see that the five required communication tools are not consistently implemented. Programs generally contain an aim and often involve some training

---

* Masaaki Imai, Kaizen Institute, "Definition of Kaizen," video, 4:52, https://www.kaizen.com/what-is-kaizen.html.

DOI: 10.4324/9781003267768-7

or an event. But they may be missing important tools or components such as standard work, reports, and key performance indicators. For example, you may find a safety program that encourages people to wear safety glasses. The program was likely started by a manager concerned with safety throughout the organization, and it probably includes some safety signs in high-traffic areas and a training session offered to the whole organization. A few people may have changed their behavior and increased their use of safety glasses, but many will continue going without safety glasses. The manager has checked the box and moved on to another program. With no feedback, reporting, or evaluation, the behavior of wearing safety glasses will not change and will remain inconsistent throughout the organization.

This safety program would be a good candidate for formalization into an improvement sub-system. Formalization will give the program a permanent place as a sub-system in the organization's improvement system and will expand the adoption of safety glasses by including the procedure in standard work that gets reviewed regularly.

You must exercise some judgment in determining which improvement efforts will benefit from formalization into a complete sub-system. In the example above, what had been a safety glasses program became standard work in a formal safety sub-system. But not every program requires or deserves the attention that formalization bestows. Programs that are intended to be temporary do not need to be formalized.

Formalized programs will be mapped individually as improvement sub-systems. To move beyond the partial efforts of a program, all components should be identified and the five communication tools should be implemented. Each organization has one improvement system encompassing many programs or sub-systems. You should be able to identify individual improvement programs (or informal sub-systems), such as 5S, coaching, problem-solving, training, or performance evaluation. To begin the work of formalizing existing programs into improvement sub-systems, start by identifying the existing efforts to improve. Once identified, an improvement system map will be created as you convert these informal programs into formal sub-systems. You will likely find a number of programs that will continue as programs.

The sub-systems team members are generally drawn from multiple areas creating a cross-functional team. As such they have fewer common experiences and may not have the same perspective. As a result, creating excellence across the organization can feel like herding cats because everyone seems to have their own way of doing things. Although creating consistent improvement across the organization is difficult, it is valuable. The improvement sub-system map provides a structure for creating lasting improvement across your organization.

As you design an improvement sub-system, you will be working to identify all components, implement the five communication tools within the subsystem, and execute across the organization. This work requires people from different areas. Since it may be difficult to envision how an existing program will be transformed into a formalized sub-system, consider the following questions an idea generation team might discuss as it works to formalize its improvement sub-system:

- Is there standard work for the idea generation cards? Do people understand what we want them to do?
- Once the idea cards are submitted, does someone respond in a timely manner? Is there an idea cards submission report?
- Are there specific idea submission goals or measurements?
- Is there a consistent review schedule that gives feedback on how they're doing?

When the design work is complete, a typical, medium-sized organization (1,000 people) is likely to have between 8 and 12 improvement sub-systems. Although you may finish with that many sub-systems, we recommend that you begin with formalizing two improvement systems. The sub-system map is detailed in the rest of the chapter.

IMPROVEMENT SUB-SYSTEM MAPS

See Figure 7.1 for improvement sub-system map example.

As you work through the map, you begin in the upper-left corner. The green-colored system information includes the system name, system leader, aim, and team members.

Improvement Sub-System Map

Improvement Sub-System	Improvement Sub-System Leader
Idea Generation	Jill

Aim

Everyone is submitting ideas for improvement

Elements

Idea generation card, Idea tracking database, idea approval process

Team Members

Gwen, Tim, Tracy, George, Sam

Standard Work	Reports
Idea Cards	Ideas Submitted
Improvement Blitz	Ideas Completed
Improvement Events	Blitz Report
	Event Report

Schedule / Cadence

Feedback	Frequency	wk1	wk2	wk3	wk4	wk5	wk6	wk7	wk8	wk9	wk10	wk11	wk12	wk13
Area Idea Review	Weekly	x	x	x	x	x	x	x	x	x	x	x	x	x
Dept. Idea Review	Monthly	x				x				x				x
Idea Gen Team Mtg	Monthly			x				x				x		
Individual Asgn Rev	Bi-weekly		x		x		x		x		x		x	

Improvement Sub-System Log

Next Action	Assign	Due	Status
Develop onboard training for new people	Tim	15-Apr	100%
Schedule blitz opportunities	Tracy	15-May	75%
Recognition proposal for top ideas	Sam	1-Jun	25%

Key Performance Indicators	Goal	Feb	Mar	Apr
Participation level by area (1 idea per month)	80%	75%	77%	72%

Key Behavioral Indicators	Status
Leaders give feedback within 2 weeks for every idea	yellow
Implemented ideas are celebrated	red
All workers know how to complete an idea card	green
Workers create solutions to problems	yellow
Solutions are immediately recorded on cards	red

FIGURE 7.1

The example improvement sub-system map shows an idea generation improvement sub-system.

System Name and Leader

The improvement sub-system map identifies the name of the improvement sub-system and the leader. Looking at this sample improvement sub-system map, you can see that Jill is the leader of the Idea Generation sub-system. Jill may be the continuous improvement manager of the organization or she may simply be someone assigned to lead the team. Part of the work of formalizing an improvement sub-system may include identifying appropriate sub-system leaders. An improvement sub-system leader can be someone from middle management who works well with work systems leaders. They can use their relationships to spread the improvement work across the whole organization.

Aim

The aim of an improvement sub-system is a statement of direction. The aim should be specific but it should not include metrics. Notice the aim in this example: Everyone is submitting ideas for improvement focused on organizational objectives and goals. This aim is clear enough to guide the work of the sub-system, yet it does not get bogged down in formulas or measurements. It is a plain language, common sense guide for the work of the sub-system. An example might be the following for a formalized 5S system: "Make things easier to find when needed without interrupting the flow of work. Keep the workplace clean and orderly so abnormal conditions become easily visible."

Sub-system Team

Sub-system team members generally come from many different parts of the organization, which creates a cross-functional team. Representatives from various work systems are chosen to be part of the improvement sub-system team. They create the standard work, review reports, and train the work system and management system leaders throughout the organization. The sub-system leader can pick work system leaders or experienced team members to be part of the sub-system team. The opportunity to be part of a sub-system team can be a good way to develop future work system leaders. Because the team is cross-functional, it can also aid in translating the sub-system in very different work environments.

Standard Work

Generally, the current state of improvement programs includes a lot of activity with very little documented standard work. But we cannot assume that members of an improvement team are on the same page if we have never created standard work. Creating standard work is an excellent way to develop the necessary dialog and input to create a standard practice throughout the organization. Standard work literally gets everyone on the same page.

The standard work listed on a sub-system map will explain how to conduct the improvement activities specific to this sub-system. This standard work is then available to each work or management system. Standard work can come in many formats: an outline, a checklist, a list of steps, directions, instructions, and plans. For example, the standard work for the idea generation sub-system includes instructions on using the idea cards and process steps for holding an improvement blitz or other improvement events.

Reports

On the improvement sub-system map, list the data created or used by the sub-system to make decisions. In the example of idea generation (see Figure 7.1), the standard work and the reports match up quite nicely: idea cards create data reported in the "Ideas Submitted" and "Ideas Completed" reports, and the improvement blitz creates data reported in a "Blitz Report." In other sub-systems that may not happen. It is not necessary to have a report for each standard work.

The sub-system team members are not likely to review reports with the frequency that work and management system team members do. In general, improvement sub-system reports are reviewed on a monthly basis. As with work systems, data presented in reports should be accurate, specific, and fit for use. Some of the data related to the improvement sub-system will be reported directly to the work systems, and thus will be listed as a report on the work system map.

Feedback

As you consider the feedback on the improvement sub-system example map, you will notice that there is considerably less feedback listed than on the work system map—only a few items per sub-system and the schedule is not as frequent. Generally, team members of each sub-system will be meeting once a month for 30 minutes to an hour to ensure that the work and management systems efforts are coordinated and represented. Much of the feedback happens in one-on-one conversations as each member works on his or her individual assignments. Individual assignment feedback sessions are held weekly or bi-weekly between the system leader and the person with the assignment.

Schedule/Cadence

The improvement sub-system map shows 13 weeks in a quarter. To schedule feedback opportunities, such as meetings, simply mark the column for each type of feedback. If a meeting is held each week, there is an X in each column. Bi-weekly meetings are marked in every other column. A monthly meeting is once per every four boxes and, if held quarterly, only one X will appear in the whole row. After the dates have passed, the map can be used to note which scheduled meetings (feedback) occurred. You can shade in the square in an electronic document to show which meetings happened. It is often easier to schedule the meetings than it is to follow through and hold them.

Improvement Log

The improvement log captures assignments related to improving the sub-system (Figure 7.2). From our example map, the monthly idea generation sub-system team meeting provides the forum for team members to discuss ideas to improve the cards, reports, and training. As the team discusses these ideas, they should make appropriate specific assignments. The assignments are recorded on the improvement log section of the map. In this map, we show the status as a percentage rather than the due date

Improvement Sub-System Log	Assign	Due	Status
Develop onboard training for new people	Tim	15-Apr	100%
Schedule blitz opportunities	Tracy	15-May	75%
Recognition proposal for top ideas	Sam	1-Jun	25%

FIGURE 7.2
The improvement log from the example map.

shown in the example work system map. Sometimes the problem with the improvement log is that the system leader does not make time to maintain it. In that case, ownership of the improvement log may be assigned to another team member.

KEY PERFORMANCE INDICATORS: WHAT TO MEASURE

The key performance indicators (KPIs) are the measurements for the sub-system. In the example, the metric being tracked is idea generation participation level by person. This objective tells how the sub-system is doing. Additional metrics, such as percent of people submitting ideas or number of ideas submitted, could be tracked as well. It is not necessary to measure everything. When considering key performance indicators, it is best to consider them carefully and find the right one. What you choose to measure will greatly influence how people think about what to do. If you were working to formalize the idea generation sub-system at your organization, you might want to consider the following:

- What will create the most meaning when measured?
- Will you count ideas submitted?
- Will you count ideas implemented?
- Will you measure levels of participation?
- How will the measurement impact behavior?

If you choose ideas submitted, does it matter how many ideas have been implemented? If you choose ideas implemented, but all of the ideas come from one or two people, is that what you want? In the example, we chose level of participation because our focus was to get as many people involved as possible, not just count how many ideas were submitted. Different organizations may have different circumstances, so they may choose different metrics to measure.

Generally, improvement sub-systems will have only a few key performance indicators. Once the metric or metrics are determined, you must determine the level of performance that will indicate success. That is your goal.

In the example map, the KPI measures participation level with a goal of 80% of people submitting three ideas per quarter. In February, the average number of people through all areas was 75%. In March, 77% participated. These key performance indicators indicate that the organization is close to its goal of 80%. Measurement can be a powerful motivational tool, but only if the team members believe that the measurement is a fair representation of their efforts.

KEY BEHAVIORAL INDICATORS: WHAT TO PRACTICE

Once you decide on the measurement, you can ask the follow-up question: what do people need to do to meet and sustain the performance expectations? What people do (actions) that will positively affect the key performance indicators are referred to as *key behavioral indicators (KBIs)*. These KBIs are the leading indicators and should predict the future results (KPIs) of a system. Systems need to be designed to drive correct behavior by making it easier to do the right things. Key behaviors need to be practiced in order to create habits. As people turn practiced behavior into habits, organizational performance will improve as a result of desired behavior moving closer to ideal and becoming deeply embedded into an organization's culture. How well the identified KBIs are improving should correlate strongly with improvement in KPIs.

Doug McIntosh, a member of the 1963-64 Bruin's NCAA national basketball championship team, explained legendary Coach John Wooden's approach to success:

> *He built great teams in practice. He was a 'practice coach,' and he conducted practices at a very high level. How you practice is how you play is what he believed. … I don't know that there was a secret to his success. It was just those three things he stressed: fundamentals, condition, and team spirit. The drills he ran at UCLA were mostly the same drills I had run back in high school—the very same drills. Coach Wooden just did them more repetitively and with more speed and precision. He just demanded a higher level of execution when it came to fundamentals. There was no secret formula.* *

---

* John Wooden and Steve Jamison, *Coach Wooden's Leadership Game Plan for Success: 12 Lessons for Extraordinary Performance and Personal Excellence* (New York, NY: McGraw-Hill Education, 2009), 250.

What prevents ideal behavior? The short answer is that we have not designed systems with focus on behaviors, rather, in many cases, we have focused solely on measurements. Generally, people do what they understand, are comfortable with, are rewarded for, and what they see will get results quickly. When people in an organization are not behaving ideally, the system team should consider adjustments to the system that will increase their ability to behave more closely to ideal behavior or that will decrease their ability to behave in an undesirable way that moves them further from ideal behavior. As stated earlier, the system should make it easy to do the right (ideal) thing, and hard to do the wrong (not ideal) thing. In this example, people will submit ideas when they anticipate that their idea will be valued. People will not submit ideas if they perceive the behavior as a waste of time. Part of designing and implementing the idea generation sub-system is creating a system that is aligned to the principles and that drives behavior closer to the ideal.

Key behavior indicators for the idea generation sub-system include:

- Leaders celebrate/recognize the person who submitted an implemented idea—perhaps taking a picture of the person who thought of an improvement when it was implemented.
- Leaders ensure that everyone understands how to correctly complete an idea submission card. (An easy way to include non-English speakers in idea generation is to use their cell phones to take pictures of problems and counter measures.)
- People document creative countermeasures on idea cards and then spread the information throughout the organization.

Key behavioral indicators do not require precise metrics (Figure 7.3). Some organizations like to use a red, yellow, green evaluation method to express trends in behavior. Evaluation can be conducted quickly to provide information for the feedback sessions. With so many behaviors contributing to each KPI, determining a KBI that correlates well with the improvement in a KPI is a critical activity and may take several rounds, especially as the culture matures.

Key behavioral indicators might be considered the secret sauce of the *Shingo Model*. Occasionally, organizations become so focused on KPIs that leaders find themselves acting as cheerleaders for improving the

Key Behavioral Indicators	Status
Leaders give feedback within 2 weeks for every idea	yellow
Implemented ideas are celebrated	red
All workers know how to complete an idea card	green
Workers create solutions to problems	yellow
Solutions are immediately recorded on cards	red

FIGURE 7.3
Key behavior indicators do not require metrics. A scale such as *green, yellow, red* or best, good, needs improvement will suffice.

numbers or nagging team members to improve performance. Many times, improvements are made but the behaviors that achieved them were less than ideal and not sustainable. These become temporary highs that are soon followed by a return to the status quo. Such a situation can be frustrating for everyone because no changes in behavior are offered. Everyone is left helpless and confused. In following the *Shingo Model* by identifying key behaviors, leaders offer something actionable, changes in behavior, to team members. Workers can practice these behaviors and in doing so influence the measurement. Thus, everyone knows what is expected and what to do to improve and succeed.

Any improvement to the entire organization must be adopted by both leaders and team members. Leaders must practice and exemplify key behaviors as much as team members. In many cases, it is the behavior of the leaders that creates the environment in the culture of an organization that enables improvement at the organization to accelerate. For example, when the idea generation sub-system team considers what can be done to generate more ideas, they will find that the behavior of the leaders in the organization is essential. When leaders review ideas regularly, quickly respond to ideas (whether accepted or not), and recognize idea implementation, team members will feel that it is worthwhile to submit improvement ideas. Leaders must also submit ideas themselves by filling out the idea generation cards. So, the behavior or the example of the organization's leaders will affect each individual who could submit ideas.

The *Shingo Guiding Principles* that inform these ideal behaviors are "lead with humility" and "respect every individual." Leaders lead by example (what they do) and not just by what they say.

AIM, KEY BEHAVIORS, AND KEY PERFORMANCE INDICATORS

There is a relationship between the aim of the sub-system—what we intend to do to achieve it (KBIs)—and how we measure performance (KPIs). The aim of the sub-system is the direction that it is heading. The aim helps us to know what to measure. For example, in an archery competition, before even lifting your bow, you must face the target and know which of the targets belongs to you.

Imagine that the team working on the idea generation sub-system determines that a needed improvement is to increase the participation of people submitting ideas. An appropriate measurement (KPI) would be the percent of people who have an idea implemented each quarter. An improvement goal would be to have 80% of people have an idea implemented each quarter.

In an archery competition, the number of holes in a target is the KPI. Or, more specifically, the KPI would be the number of holes made in each ring of the target.

However, as you strive to improve the KPI measures, it is not all that helpful to simply tell people to shoot more shots in the bullseye. What will really help is to identify the key behaviors and then to practice them. Often, when the goals are not achieved, the organization falls back to cheerleading and nagging. But the real need is to identify and refine the behaviors.

For many people, it is much easier to identify things to measure than it is to carefully identify how the system aligns people's behavior to the ideal behavior informed by the guiding principles (Figure 7.4). As you formalize the improvement system at your organization, it is best to identify the specific key behavioral indicators that will affect the key performance indicators. In archery, the way to get more arrows closer to the bullseye is to carefully execute the shot. The key behaviors to improve your score would be to:

- Properly align your sights.
- Hold your breath while releasing the string.
- Release the string smoothly with no quick jerks.

Each of these behaviors will affect the arrow's placement in the target. Together, these behaviors will determine your score. In order to improve performance, you must improve the behaviors that contribute most to the measurement of success.

FIGURE 7.4
Direction (aim) and behavior (KBI) are the foundation of any score or measurement.

If they are not making progress, many people will simply measure differently. However, all things remaining the same, changing what you measure will not get you any closer to perfection. The real solution for lasting improvement is to identify the ideal behaviors that a system needs to align to and formalize the sub-system to drive that behavior toward the ideal. If you don't know, then you can observe and experiment until you find the key behaviors contributing to or hindering performance.

ORGANIZATION-WIDE IMPROVEMENT

Improvement activity often grows organically. It starts in one work system where it may be fine-tuned and spread to other work systems. Eventually, with effort, a good method may spread throughout the company. The job of an improvement sub-system team is to identify best practices and help spread them throughout the organization. Some organizations even build an improvement sub-system to spread knowledge and best practices across the entire company.* The purpose of formalizing improvement sub-systems is to increase the speed of implementation throughout the whole organization.

---

* Often called "knowledge sharing" or *yokoten* systems.

8

Management Systems

The management systems optimize the whole organization by strengthening the connections and communication within and between all systems. The management systems are the responsibility of executives or upper-level management of the organization. Such senior leaders have two jobs: to lead the organization and to improve the organization. A significant part of this effort is accomplished by developing system leaders in all systems.

The Shingo systems design approach strives to improve connections and communication. The term *management system* can have many meanings. It can refer to the overall management of the organization and it can refer to upper-level or executive managers. In the systems design model, the management systems that we are referring to are those systems that provide direction and alignment to the work systems and improvement systems. Based on the size of the organization, these management systems could be at the top level of the organization or in middle management. It is not necessary (and very difficult) to define all levels of management in the initial stages of system design. The focus in the beginning is to identify those leaders who provide direction to the work and improvement systems.

Before an organization formalizes management system components, an informal business management methodology already exists in the organization. The initial purpose of formalizing a management system is to align the activities of the organization. This is done by developing leaders of work systems and improvement sub-systems. The scope of a management system is to lead and align the organization through effective systems and to improve the organization by developing the leaders of the work systems and improvement sub-systems.

DOI: 10.4324/9781003267768-8

It is impossible to develop and define all systems at the same time. In reality, it will take a few years to formalize all of the systems throughout the organization. Begin formalizing efforts by developing one management system at a time. Even more than work systems and improvement sub-systems, the formalizing of management systems will need time for the people who make up the systems to adapt to consistently using the five system communication tools. Initially, the scope of a management system should be limited to improving the organization. As the people at the organization gain confidence in the power of the five tools, the system design methodology will expand to all systems.

Because management systems strengthen the connections among the other systems, formalization generally occurs after the work and improvement systems are well developed. Management systems need to provide direction and alignment to the leaders of the work systems and the improvement sub-systems. Sometimes the upper management of an organization has little or no regular contact with work system leaders or improvement sub-system leaders. One benefit of defining management systems is the resulting regular communication between upper management and leaders at other levels of the organization. Formalizing the systems provides a common language to all levels of the organization.

System leaders on different levels of the organization need to collaborate. Formalizing the management systems by completing the management system maps assigns responsibility and facilitates communication. Regardless of differences, all system leaders can discuss their system with confidence and skill. The beauty and the magic of system maps is that they are able to work equally well in very divergent areas. The opportunity of formalizing management systems through the Shingo system design maps is to create connections through the many work and improvement systems so that each system is contributing in the best way to the overall organization.

The Shingo system map is a tool to facilitate leader development. By establishing a common vocabulary of systems and structure for discussing improvements, problems, and challenges, the Shingo approach to system design facilitates improved communication. Expanding communication between executives/upper leaders and midlevel managers to include all five system communication tools reduces the stress of unclear expectations. Measurements are important, but upper management is often not specific about what needs to be done to improve the measurements. Regular, predictable opportunities for upper and middle management to discuss the system map and the five tools can greatly reduce the stress involved in a supervisor and upper manager meeting because both will know what will be discussed and they can have confidence that they will work together to improve the area. Focusing on the five tools is less threatening than a primary focus on performance measurements.

Executives are under pressure to achieve the measurements that are assigned in their areas of responsibility. In many cases, these measurements end up focusing on individual units and do not promote collaboration between the units. It is not uncommon for the production areas of the company to be measured differently from the sales side or the finance areas. One of the goals of creating a management system map is to fine-tune the measurements to drive collaboration and optimization of the whole organization, not just the optimization of an individual area.

Noted management scholar Dr. Barbara Berry summarized Dr. Deming's ideas as follows:

> *Industrial-style thinking has led to management styles of command and control. The industrial age influenced the workplace and schools to encourage individual completeness, absolute authority, and one right–answer thinking. A change in philosophy requires unlearning industrial thinking evident in departmentalization, scarcity of knowledge, and information competitiveness.*

> *The industrial model discourages creativity and cooperative skills. Therefore, training in creativity, communication, and interpersonal skills may be necessary …*

> *Optimization of a system can occur when all interconnecting components are orchestrated to achieve the organization's goal. The people, free of fear and competition within the system can band together for optimization of the system. In a quality system, everybody gains. The traditional "management by objectives" philosophy fails to orchestrate the components, leaving each one to do a job separate from the other components and often causing them to work against the successes of others …*

> *Competitiveness within the system leads to loss for the system.**

* Barbara Berry, *There Is a Relationship between Systems Thinking and W. Edwards Deming's Theory of Profound Knowledge* (Tulsa, OK: The Berrywood Group, Inc., 2006).

MANAGEMENT SYSTEM MAP

Note that work systems and improvement sub-systems are listed in Figure 8.1. These are the specific systems that the hypothetical management system leader, Brent Smith, will work with to strengthen communication and collaboration. The management system leader will specifically be working to provide direction to the leaders by answering the following questions:

- How much time should each leader spend on improvement?
- Have the five communication tools been well defined?
- How is each system improving?
- What are the system measurements?
- How often are the system maps reviewed?

The number of management systems depends largely on the size of the organization. A medium-size organization will have between five and ten management systems.

Leader

The leader of a management system will be an upper-level manager. Depending on the organization, this may be the plant manager, a department head, or a senior executive. The management system leader will be a decision maker for a business unit, such as a steering committee member or a division head. Initially, it is not necessary to have a management system map for each layer of management. Although, ideally, you would have one.

In the Shingo system design approach, the job of the CEO is to provide the resources necessary for those management system leaders. These resources include time to develop the five communication tools. This means that leaders have time to create and audit standard work, ensure that data and reports are in fit-for-use condition, give personal feedback on a regular basis, and capture improvement opportunities in an improvement log.

Management System Map

Management System:	Operations					Leader:	Brent
Aim:	To develop system leaders within my scope of leadership						

Management Systems	Leader	Work Systems	Leader	Improvement Sub-Systems	Leader	Standard Work	Reports
Maintenance	Kim	Metal Fabrication	George	Idea Generation	Mary		Production
Purchasing	Shaun	Powder Coating	Mary	5S	Juan		Shipping
Manufacturing	Tina	Packaging	Edgar	Problem Solving	Susan		Maintenance
		Assembly	Juan	Quality	Sam		Budget
		Shipping	Amy				Financial
							System Map Assessments

Feedback	Schedule	wk1	wk2	wk3	wk4	wk5	wk6	wk7	wk8	wk9	wk10	wk11	wk12
Executive Committee	Bi-weekly	X		X	X		X	X	X		X		X
Go & Observe	Bi-weekly		X	X	X	X	X	X	X	X	X	X	X
Measurement Review	Monthly		X				X				X		
Financial Review	Monthly		X				X				X		
Strategic Plan Review	Quarterly			X									
System Review	Quarterly							X					

Management System Improvement Log

	Assign	Due
Create staff meeting agendas to keep meetings on time	Sam	11-Nov
Review management system with CEO	Brent	21-Oct
Schedule quarterly all-hands-on-deck meeting	Mary	25-Nov
System map training for all work system leaders	George	27-Oct
Create quality metric for purchasing	Shaun	1-Dec

Key Behavioral Indicators

	Status
Lockout Tagout training in all areas	yellow
Measuring device calibration audit	red
Schedule three kaizen events	green
Improve same-day shipment for online orders	yellow
Research transportation options with new employees	yellow
Schedule and complete feedback reviews	yellow

Key Performance Indicators (monthly)

	Goal	Oct.	Nov.	Dec.
Safety (days between incidents)	0	1	3	2
Quality (first yield)	95%	90%	94%	93%
Labor Cost Savings	-5%	-2%	-1%	-4%
Delivery (on-time shipment)	98%	96%	99%	97%
Morale (attendance—here or excused %)	75%	70%	72%	72%

Key Performance Indicators (quarterly)

	Goal	Q2	Q3	Q4
System maps reviewed this quarter	90%	70%	80%	85%

FIGURE 8.1

This management system map shows an operations management system.

The management system leader provides direction for defining systems and creating system maps. In the example management system map, Brent is the management system leader.

Aim

As you can see from the example, the aim of this Operations management system is to lead the organizational areas covered by the system through developing system leaders. An important part of this effort is implementing the five system communication tools. Brent Smith will use the same five tools (standard work, reports, feedback, schedule, and improvement log) in his work with the system leaders as they use in their systems. Brent will model how to use the tools to the system leaders. They will all have a common systems language because they are all using the same tools. In this way, coordination in the system is increased.

MULTIPLE SYSTEM RESPONSIBILITIES ON ONE MAP

A management system map is a chart of a manager's responsibility. One manager will likely oversee work systems, improvement sub-systems, and possibly some management systems. Our example map shows this manager overseeing three management systems, five work systems, and four improvement sub-systems.

A manager may also be directly responsible for creating a high-level work system, such as financial reports or business development. This work system may consist of a small cross-functional team of high-level leaders. Such a work system would still be mapped in its own work system map. If Brent from our example map were head of a Business Development work system, it would be listed on the management system map as shown in Figure 8.2.

Standard Work

Although each work and improvement sub-system listed in the management system map has standard work, the standard work listed here is only the standard work that applies to Brent's efforts to lead. Examples

Management System Map				
			Leader:	Brent
ıders within my scope of leadership				
Work Systems	Leader	Improvement Sub-Systems	Leader	
Metal Fabrication	George	Idea Generation	Mary	Leader
Powder Coating	Mary	5S	Juan	
Packaging	Edgar	Problem Solving	Susan	
Assembly	Juan	Quality	Sam	
Shipping	Amy			
Business Development	Brent			

FIGURE 8.2

In some cases, an upper-level manager will be responsible for both a management system and a work system within the management system. In that case, the upper-level manager's name appears both as the management system map leader and as a leader of a work system. This inset shows that Brent is the leader of the Business Development work system.

of standard work for an upper-level leader are leader standard work and standard work for community relations.

Reports

In many organizations, managers have developed sophisticated reports. The reports are necessary for the manager to speak in specifics with the leaders being developed. In the example, Brent will receive five operational reports: production, shipping, maintenance, budget, and financial. In addition to operational reports, system reports will need to be developed. Examples of system reports might include current system maps, system map assessments, improvement-related reports (idea generation and kaizen), improvement training, and improvement projects. Reports in a management system will have a wider view than reports for a work system or improvement sub-system.

System reports will help the managers and leaders focus their system improvement efforts.

Feedback and Schedule

The cadence of management system feedback is different from a work system, where feedback is needed daily or weekly. Management feedback occurs periodically: bi-weekly, monthly, or quarterly. Although the feedback does not occur as often as feedback in a work system, the in-person feedback is nonetheless ideal. Feedback is not just reviewing the data contained in the reports, it is reviewing the data together.

The sample map shows the dual-use nature of the schedule: Xs mark the date that the feedback is scheduled, and gray coloring of the box shows which of the scheduled feedback sessions occurred. The sample map shows a perfect quarter when all scheduled feedback is held. If a feedback session was not held, its box would be left blank. In this example, the map shows markings completed through the end of the quarter. The example map is scheduled for a system map review to be held in a few weeks.

Improvement Log

Items listed in the improvement log of the management system are unique to the management system. The management system log does not repeat the items listed in the improvement log of the work systems and improvement sub-systems. A management system improvement log contains assignments to improve the management system. A management system improvement log can also include projects (something that will take months and many people to accomplish).

Items listed in the management system improvement log are the primary focus of quarterly system reviews where the improvement log is used to clarify assignments, assign projects, and acknowledge accomplishments and status. Note the person responsible for the item in the improvement log and the due date.

KEY PERFORMANCE INDICATORS

A KPI is an output that can be measured, counted, and visualized with an associated goal. The example map shows the organization's measurements of safety, quality, labor cost savings, delivery, and morale. When determining the measures to use make sure that they matter to the customer.

One focus of the management system is the development of work system and improvement system leaders. This brings us to the question: what are the key performance indicators for leadership development? Some, but not all, organizations have highly developed management training programs. Often, organizations lack a systematic approach to management training

Key Performance Indicators (monthly)	Goal	Oct.	Nov.	Dec.
Safety (days between incidents)	0	1	3	2
Quality (first yield)	95%	90%	94%	93%
Labor Cost Savings	-5%	-2%	-1%	-4%
Delivery (on-time shipment)	98%	96%	99%	97%
Morale (attendance—here or excused %)	75%	70%	72%	72%
Key Performance Indicators (quarterly)	Goal	Q2	Q3	Q4
System maps reviewed this quarter	90%	70%	80%	85%

FIGURE 8.3

The key performance indicators and key behavioral indicators sections of the management system map.

because they are so focused on day-to-day operations. A good indication of a lack of focus on leadership development is that no KPIs are identified for leadership development. One of the strengths of the system design approach is that it is useful in identifying gaps. In the example management system map, the KPIs for the operations management system are safety, quality, labor cost savings, deliver, morale, and system maps reviewed this quarter (Figure 8.3).

KEY BEHAVIORAL INDICATORS

KBIs are the behaviors (or what you need to do) to impact the key performance indicators.

KEY BEHAVIORAL INDICATORS: LEADERSHIP

Use own management system map. (Lead by example.)
Identify gaps in leadership skills. Work to close leadership skills gaps.
Train and assist system leaders in the development of system maps.

CONCLUSION

The development of system maps, including the management system, will usually follow these phases:

1. Define the system by completing system map documentation.

2. Audit all system communication tools (standard work, reports, schedule, feedback, and improvement log).
3. Reduce variation in all components of the system.
4. Achieve a stable system reflected in the KPIs and KBIs as variation is reduced.

Management system maps are basically an outline of the management systems, work systems, and the improvement system that are owned by a specific manager. While it may take a few months to formalize a management system map, the process should not be tedious. It takes more time to develop and formalize the related work systems and improvement sub-systems, which should be done prior to formalization of the management system.

A manager could be tempted to skip the step of creating a management system map with the assumption that they are already doing the things that are on the map. Before you discount the power of the management system map, try it.

Communication is hard work.* Based on many years of diverse business experience, business author and consultant Jonathan Halls wisely claims that good communication results from "careful planning, practice, and review." The basic aim of system design is to improve communication. The Shingo system maps provide a structured format for visualizing, planning, practicing, reviewing, and improving systems.

With the management system maps complete, you can experience how the five system communication tools, when consistently employed in all three essential systems, create regular opportunities for communication and collaboration.

---

* Jonathan Halls, "Communication is Hard Work" (blog), September 14, 2017, https://jonathanhalls .com/2017/09/14/communication-is-hard-work.

9

Case Studies

Now that you have an understanding of how the five required communication tools are integrated into Shingo system maps representing the three essential systems, it may be useful to consider how two successful companies have applied this system design approach. The following case studies include samples of the actual documents the organizations used as they designed their systems.

O.C. TANNER CASE STUDY

Company Overview

With some 1,600 employees, O.C. Tanner develops strategic employee recognition and reward solutions that help people accomplish and appreciate great work. As a recipient of the Shingo Prize in 1999, O.C. Tanner has been implementing the *Shingo Model* by embedding the Shingo Guiding Principles and identifying systems for many years. The organization's list of improvement systems has been displayed on its strategy wall for more than ten years. O.C. Tanner frequently conducts tours of its Prize-recipient facilities and has hosted many Shingo workshops.

Three Essential Systems

Before participating in the pilot round of the Shingo SYSTEMS DESIGN workshop, O.C. Tanner had identified improvement systems and assigned system owners. The system owners had created one-page summaries and

DOI: 10.4324/9781003267768-9

PowerPoint slides to define and explain their system to others. The one-page summary consisted of the system name, purpose, and process (i.e., standard work recorded in a Word document). The PowerPoint contained the purpose, process, and impact of the system formatted for presentation to a group. Prior to the SYSTEMS DESIGN workshop, system owners at O.C. Tanner were left to their own judgment to determine how to complete these two documents and define their systems.

Tolan Brown, vice president of operations at O.C. Tanner, describes their journey of formalization:

> Before we started working with Brent, we were trying to get our arms around the systems. The system owners created PowerPoint presentations as a tool to teach others about their system. Just saying to someone, 'Create a PowerPoint explaining your system' doesn't work really well. Everyone approached it differently and we ended up in very different spots. I think the process of formalizing it all and using the documentation helped us to know what we need to work on and identify what we know and what we don't know.*

O.C. Tanner system leaders met to share and discuss their system PowerPoint slides, one-page summaries, and their work to complete the Shingo system maps. Together, they added to the previously identified improvement systems by organizing work cells into the following work systems:

- Delivery
- Distribution fulfillment
- Purchasing
- Logistics
- Building maintenance and tech
- International purchasing/gift cards
- Customer awards
- Production scheduling
- Product development

* Tolan Brown and David Siebert, interview by Brent Allen and April Bosworth, September 17, 2020.

- Manufacturing engineering
- Pressed product

As the O.C. Tanner team applied the common vocabulary used in Shingo systems design, they recognized that their functional units of Distribution Operations and Manufacturing Operations were management systems. Completing the management system maps fine-tuned the existing functional units.

At the beginning of the system formalization process, Tolan Brown and David Siebert, vice president of manufacturing/supply chain, both conferred with the system owners together. This executive cooperation helped ensure organizational cohesion in the adoption of the Shingo System Maps.

Siebert describes some discoveries made through formalizing: "We had some systems that we thought were systems, but they were not. The process of defining and mapping helped us determine that we should make a defined system and manage it intentionally versus just letting it happen."*

Five Required Communication Tools

All of the systems benefited from better definition of the five communication tools as the Shingo system maps were completed. Formalizing the systems illuminated excellent existing practices—most systems had appropriate and applicable reports and regular feedback was scheduled as monthly scorecard reviews. However, the process of completing the Shingo system maps showed that they had work to do in creating standard work for many of the improvement sub-systems and that a system review, apart from the system metrics, was not happening on a consistent basis. After an initial round of feedback, in which system leaders presented their maps to each other, the maps will undergo a quarterly review cycle.

Formalization Challenges

The biggest challenge of formalization for O.C. Tanner was determining what kind of system map to complete. Some systems were difficult to assign to one type of system map. For example, some would put strategy

---

* Brown and Siebert, interview, September 17, 2020.

deployment as a management system and others thought of it as an improvement sub-system. After discussing it for a while, they decided to pick one, complete the map, and see what they could learn.

Results of System Mapping (KBI/KPI Improvements)

After almost a year into its journey with the Shingo system maps, Siebert described the organization's current way of tracking results: "We have a score card that we use every month already in place. It's really identifying key performance indicators for the various systems and tracking them."[*]

Looking forward, Brown predicts:

> I think as we go deeper and continue to refine the systems, we'll probably add things or change things on those score cards. We'll realize that there are systems not adequately measuring their performance, so we'll probably tweak our score card.[†]

We recommended that they add two new measurements to their scorecards: "system maps completed" and "system reviews completed." These measurements can be measured quarterly and will provide the necessary visibility to the system design process.

Table 9.1 shows the systems that O.C. Tanner has identified and begun to formalize according to the ideas of Shingo system design.

O.C. Tanner's System Design Maps

Figures 9.1–9.3 are examples of O.C. Tanner's maps completed by system owners. First is a management system map for the Distribution Operations management system. Following that is a work system map for the delivery system. And the third map is an improvement sub-system map for the 5S improvement sub-system. Note that O.C. Tanner highlights a cell in blue to draw attention to items that are currently being worked on.

---

[*] Brown and Siebert, interview, September 17, 2020.
[†] Brown and Siebert, interview, September 17, 2020.

Systems at O.C. Tanner	
Work Systems	**Improvement Sub-systems**
Distribution	5S
Purchasing	Abnormality
International Purchasing	Problem Solving
Logistics	Process Standard Work
Maintenance	Hiring
Research and Development	Environmental
Pressed Product	Safety
Custom Product	Gemba
Build Engineering	Delivery System
Production Sched./Systems	Coaching
	Strategy Development, part 1
Management Systems	Strategy Development, part 2
Manufacturing Operations	Quality
Distribution Operations	Standardized Work
	Team Meetings & Huddles
	Visual Management
	Operations Training

TABLE 9.1

After six months of work to formalize systems as presented in this book, O.C. Tanner had identified and begun work on 10 work systems, 17 improvement sub-systems, and 2 management systems

Lessons Learned

According to Brown, "one of the biggest benefits of the process was identifying our strengths and weaknesses system by system."[*]

Landon Kleeme, operations group leader and training manager, has assisted many of his fellow system owners in creating their maps. He says:

> *I think that one of the benefits of the map has been that it made you stop and really think a little bit deeper about your work. When I was creating my map, there were parts of my system that I didn't really realize were part of the system. I wasn't really managing them very well. I feel like it encouraged and pushed me toward a deeper understanding of my system.*[†]

---

[*] Brown and Siebert, interview, September 17, 2020.
[†] Tolan Brown, Landon Kleeme, and David Siebert, interview by Brent Allen and April Bosworth, February 2, 2021.

Management System Map

Management System:	Distribution Operations		Leader:	David Siebert
Aim:	Deliver on time, 100% quality while reducing costs. Ensure our offerings are a competitive advantage - Develop people ?			

Work Systems	Leader	Improvement Systems	Leader	Standard Work	Reports	Assign	Due
Distribution	Nermana	5S	Phil	Leaders std work	Purchasing report		
Purchasing	Robin	Abnormalities	Benita	System quarterly review	Backlog		
International Purchasing	Seth	Problem solving	Nate	Standard meetings	Maint. report		
Logistics	Mike	Process support	Josh		Score card review		
Maintenance	Ron	Hiring	Janet				
		Environmental	Annette				
		Safety	Hanh				
		Gemba	Benita				
		Delivery system	Dave / Mindy				
		Coaching	Adam				
		Strategy Deployment (2 parts)	Shane / Seth B				
		Quality System	Nermana				

Feedback (5)	Schedule	4/6	4/13	4/20	4/27	5/4	5/11	5/18	5/25	6/1	6/8	6/15	6/22	6/29
Daily Huddle (5)	Daily	X	X	X	X	X	X	X	X	X	X	X	X	X
Distribution leadership	Bi-weekly	X	X	X	X	X	X	X	X	X	X	X	X	X
Distribution staff	Bi-weekly		X	X	X	X	X	X	X		X			
Gary Staff meeting	Weekly	X	X	X	X	X	X	X	X	X	X	X	X	X
Results review Purchasing	Monthly	X	X	X	X	X	X	X	X	X	X	X	X	X
Results Int.Purchasing	Monthly	?												
Coaching (5)	Weekly	X	X	X	X	X	X	X	X	X	X	X	X	X
Financial Review	Monthly	X	X					X				X		X
Systems Review (Devel Tolar	Monthly	?												
Imp. System Review	Monthly	?												
Scorecard review	Monthly	?												

Management System Improvement Log	Assign	Due
Distribution work system map	Nermana	May 20th
Need to clarify MESH and Environmental	Annette	

Key Performance Indicators	Goal	Jan.	Feb.	March	April	May	June
	Cheryls report						

Key Behavioral Indicators

Safety (4)	
Quality (3)	
Delivery (4)	
Cost (3)	
Morale (1)	
5S	

FIGURE 9.1

Before attempting to customize the Shingo system design maps, O.C. Tanner formalized systems in the form suggested in this book. They wanted to be sure they had learned all they could from the provided materials before making customizations.

Work System Map

		A/B	C/D		E	F/G	H		Schedule													

Work System	Work System Leader	Feedback	Frequency	6/1	6/8	6/15	6/22	6/29	7/6	7/13	7/20	7/27	8/3	8/10	8/17	8/24	8/31
Delivery system	Dave Siebert / Mindy Murano	Team QED reports	Daily	x	x	x	x	x	x	x	x	x	x	x	x	x	x
Aim		Interactives	Daily	x	x	x	x	x	x	x	x	x	x	x	x	x	x
Deliver orders on time to our customers both internal and external.		Trends Dashboard	Real time	x	x	x	x	x	x	x	x	x	x	x	x	x	x
		Client Exp Scorecard	Monthly								x					x	
Workflows		Delivery Status report	Daily	x	x	x	x	x	x	x	x	x	x	x	x	x	x
ZSEQ, Team Interactives, QED daily reports, Client Experience Scorecard		Summary report	Qtly	x	x												

Team Members

Team Members 500+ (Team leaders (50+), Group leaders (20+), Directors (8), VP's (2), EVP -- Client success, Client experience

Standard Work	Reports	Imp. Systems	Work System improvement Log	Assign	Due
Scheduling / Lunching	ZSEQ	5S	UK on time - questions on the best way to measure as orders can be late from US teams	Dave	6/15
Ineractive	ZMFGINT Interactive 3X day	Abnormalities	Need to get drop ships working	Darin	6/15
QED reports	Team boards - QED	Problem solving	Next steps to not doing Delivery status report	Dave	
	Client Exp. Scorecard	Process support			
	Delivery status	Hiring			
		Environmental			
		Safety			
		Gemba			
		Delivery system			
		Coaching			
		Strategy Deployment (2parts)			
		Quality System			

Key Performance Indicators	Goal	July	Aug	Sept	Oct	Nov	Dec	Key Behavioral Indicators
On time delivery	98%+	Refer to scorecard	Refer to scorecard					
		Refer to scorecard	Refer to scorecard					
		Refer to scorecard	Refer to scorecard					

FIGURE 9.2

O.C. Tanner Work System Map with blue highlighted items.

Improvement System Map

Improvement System	Improvement System Leader		Schedule / Cadence												
			wk 1	wk 2	wk 3	wk 4	wk 5	wk 6	wk 7	wk 8	wk 9	wk 10	wk 11	wk 12	wk 13
5S	Phillip Child														

	Feedback	Frequency	wk 1	wk 2	wk 3	wk 4	wk 5	wk 6	wk 7	wk 8	wk 9	wk 10	wk 11	wk 12	wk 13
	Quarterly Launch Meeting	Quarterly		X			X			X				X		
	Quarter Report Published	Quarterly			X			X			X				X	

Aim

In a world of rapid and continuous changes, our company must continuously improve in order to survive and be successful. With its focus on being clean and organized, 5S helps prepare us as individuals, and our environment for improvement.

Major Elements

Google docs which inclues Audit froms, routes of 5S audits, list of auditors, and historical audits.

Team Members

Team Members 500+: (Team leaders (50+), Group leaders (20+), Directors 8), VP's (2), EVP (1)

Standard Work	Reports	Management Systems
Audit form	QTRY report	Operations
Meeting with auditors	QTR Meeting	Distribution Operations
New 5S training packet		Manufacturing Operations
Audit Standards		

Improvement System Log

Next Action	Assigned to	Due	status
Better way to store documents (Teams discussion on 6/8/2020) waiting for feedback	Mike		
Waiting SCS team SCS-6568 to be prioritized with FL and when SCS is ready.			Done
1/11/2021 updated last quarter's scores	Phil	01/11/21	X
Realign all the audits since Emblem moves at the end of 2020	Phil	02/15/21	
Training of new 5S auditors	Phil	01/12/21	

Key Performance Indicators	Goal	QTR 1	QTR 2	QTR 3 2020	QTR 4 2020
Overall 5S Score	B+ 3.3	B 3.0	B 3.2	B+ 3.2	B+ 3.3
5S Certification in Bridge	96.00%				

Key Behavioral Indicators	Goal	Actual
Gemba Pass Rate	95%	94.00%

FIGURE 9.3

While the forms consolidating the five required communication tools and reflecting the unique qualities of the three types of essential systems were new to O.C. Tanner, they had identified the systems, especially the improvement sub-systems, of their organization years before.

LIFETIME PRODUCTS CASE STUDY

Company Overview

Lifetime Products builds durable quality products for consumers and their families. It employs 2,500 people in the United States. Lifetime Products is a pioneer of the system map approach. The management team of Lifetime Products learned about the *Shingo Model* in depth in an exclusive training with Jacob Raymer in 2012. Following a challenge from Raymer, a team worked to figure out what systems meant at Lifetime Products. They focused first on defining work systems. After thoughtful discussion and experimentation, the forerunner to the Shingo system maps presented in this book were implemented throughout the US facilities. Regular contact and discussion between leaders and workers about systems has become a basis of the culture at Lifetime Products.

Nate McConkie, director of accounting, who also functions as the continuous improvement manager at Lifetime Products, describes the value of system design:

> *I think the biggest value is the constant touch points. I think challenging the leadership of Lifetime to think about their work in a meaningful way provides the majority of the value. We are doing either quarterly assessments or reviews,* but they accomplish the same thing. They *check to make sure that the system is not stagnant. We're continually finding gaps in the systems.*[†]

Challenges and Solutions of Implementation

McConkie recalls the process of completing a system map as a system owner a few years ago. He says:

> *I think it helped elevate everybody's understanding of why we're doing system maps. Once we understood that, some of the other parts of the work system gave benefit as we started to learn how to use them.*

---

[*] An explanation of the system reviews and system assessments mentioned here is given later in this chapter.
[†] Nate McConkie interview by Brent Allen and April Bosworth, October 13, 2020.

> *Standard work, for example—being forced to write our processes down into a map—also forced us to generate printable standard work instead of a tribal standard work. That benefit came probably a year and a half later.** *

When asked what the current system owners find most difficult about sustaining systems at Lifetime Products, McConkie responded, "[Being asked to] put your job into these predefined squares on this Excel document."[†]

You may have expected that resistance to the unknown would diminish after your initial rollout of system maps, but as McConkie points out, any time a new person becomes a system owner you are likely to find similar hesitancy. Regardless of your stage in the process, the way to overcome resistance to system maps is to start using them.

> *Regardless of your stage in the process, the way to overcome resistance to system maps is to start using them.*

Sustaining the System Mapping Project

While many system owners are independent in holding regular system reviews, a few system owners require a reminder from McConkie to schedule system reviews or assessments. Several years into system maps, McConkie reports that "about seventy-five percent are using that improvement log. We're documenting anything that's coming out of that review as action items on that improvement log."[‡] Current improvement logs indicate active systems.

Systems at Lifetime Products

Tables 9.2 and 9.3 show the systems that Lifetime Products has identified.

---

* McConkie, interview, October 13, 2020.
† McConkie, interview, October 13, 2020.
‡ McConkie, interview, October 13, 2020.

Management Systems and Improvement Sub-systems at Lifetime Products

Management Systems	Planning/Control
Human Resources	Purchasing
Manufacturing Process	Quality
Metals	Sales
Plastics	Accounting
Manufacturing Engineering	Marketing
Maintenance	Logistics
Product Development	**Improvement Sub-systems**
Information Technology	Strategy Deployment
Legal	Systems Development

TABLE 9.2

After five years of applying systemic thinking, lifetime products has formalized 17 management systems and 2 improvement sub-systems

Work Systems at Lifetime Products

Packaging/ boards	Change Management	Expediting
Sheds	Project Management	Shipping
Fabrication	Product Testing	Transportation
Powder Coating	IT Operations	Transportation
Manufacturing Materials	Software Development	Purchasing
Playsets and Coolers	DB/Infrastructure	FG Inventory
H-3 Production	EDI	Dispatch
Metals Materials	Telecommunications	Sales Management
Blow Molding	Legal	Customer Service
Plastics SMED	Master Scheduling	Direct Sales
Plastics Materials	Sales and Operation	Lifetime Retail Stores
New Equipment	Planning	Customer Service
Deployment	Production (Purchasing)	Shipping
Automation and	MRO Purchasing	Marketing
Controls	International Sourcing	Human Resources
Tooling	Manufacturing Quality	Safety
Machine Shop	PC Quality	Payroll/HRIS
Equipment Maintenance	Metals Quality	Accounts Receivable
Facility Maintenance	Plastics Quality	Accounts Payable
House Keeping	Receiving Quality	General Ledger
Tool Crib	Packaging Design	Tax
Design (Product)	Traffic	Financial Reporting

TABLE 9.3

Lifetime products has formalized 66 work systems

Lifetime Products System Maps

Figures 9.4–9.6 are three sample system maps by Lifetime Products: a work system map with improvement log, an improvement sub-system map with improvement log, and a management system map.

You'll notice that the system maps used at Lifetime Products have a slightly different look than the ones you've seen in this book. For example, the improvement log sits to the side for the work and improvement sub-systems and the Excel document includes additional sections for training plan and auditing plan. Also, the *Shingo Model* color coding has not been implemented. Finally, management systems at Lifetime Products are organized by executive level leaders.

Formal System Feedback

Over the years, Lifetime has developed two ways of giving formal feedback to the work system leaders. The first method is called a "system assessment," and it includes specific metrics. The second method is called a "review." It focuses on needed improvement rather than a value judgement of the system. Both feedback methods are described here.

System Assessment

Procedures: A work system assessment is conducted by an assessor who is not part of the work system. The assessor chooses a person in the work system and asks questions about the components of the system. Assessments are scheduled by system leaders.

Documents: The work system assessment is an Excel form with a checklist of questions that match each portion of the system map. The form contains detailed descriptions of how and why to conduct the assessment (Figure 9.7).

System Review

Procedures: A work system review is conducted by work system leaders who are outside of the system being reviewed.

Work System:	Transportation	Work System Leader:	Amy Nichols

Work System Purpose (What We Do)

Business Systems: Logistics

Work System Goal or Objective: Effectively and safely improve the movement of product through the Freeport center and along the Wasatch front to lifetime customers.

Measurement	Formulas
Kaizens	Total kaizens/ month
Accidents/Incidents	Total Injuries/ Incidents/ Month
Hours worked	Hours worked

System users

Supervisor
Leads
Employees

Line Item Objectives: (How We Do It-Broken Down)

Effective communication by strong process 1
Documented UDOT Compliance 2
Standard Safe Driving practices 3
On Time delivery 4
Accurate trailer moves to eliminate waiting & rework 5
Execute a daily document truck schedule 6
Improve Mentoring 7

Standard Work Groups (How We Know What To DO)	**Reports**	**Lean Tools**
Daily vehicle inspections process	Inspection books	Kaizen
Cleaning Visual	DOT files	Visual/5s
YMS Visual	Yard management system YMS	Standardized work
Reporting maintenance issues	Kizan	
Load delivery verification process	Safety	Stop and fix
Delivery confirmation process	Truck manger system TMS	Coaching

Training Plan (How To Train)	**Auditing Plan** (How We Audit)
New hire training only when we have new hires.	Weekly equipment inspection spot checks, 2X weekly OTR load securement inspection,1X quarterly Hostler safety audit. We go over inspection logs daily. Each standard work process will be done quarterly bases
1/2 hour monthly training have employees do a safety training with group daily.	

Date	Work System Improvement Log	Status
07/28/16	Review System map with Wes	Done
07/29/16	reviewing and showing Michael how to read and use standardized work	Done
07/29/16	updated tools Yard management system	Done
07/29/16	updating auditing plan / added go inspections daily	Done
07/29/16	updated Measurement's	Done
07/29/16	reviewing and showing Robert how to read and use standardized work	Done
08/03/16	changed audit planning for hostlers	Done
08/05/16	training plan on new hires	Done
08/09/16	review with Brent and Wes	Done
08/09/16	mentoring team kizan event	Done
08/09/16	review driver check list	Done
09/02/16	the work system to make sure were following everything	Done
09/08/16	Aaron and I going over my work system to better align item with objectives with measurement's	Done
9/8/2016	Roger and Wes going over the work system auditing with me.	Done
09/08/16	need to add and change work system purpose	Done
09/08/16	we numbered the objectives and measurement's so the work system makes system.	Done
09/08/16	cleaning up tools area	Done
	Auditing plan needing updated	Done
09/09/16	Brent and Wes myself going over and reviewing the work system map.	Done
09/14/16	Robert and I training on the work system map	Done
09/15/16	adding lean tools	Done
09/19/16	training the area on work system purpose,Objectives,measurements	Done
10/05/16	going over processes with employee	Done
10/13/16	going over work system with Bob getting ready for the next review	Done
10/26/16	going over work system map with Joe cross	Done
10/31/16	being auditing on the work system map. Wes Roger Bob	Done
10/31/16	outline the purpose in red to highlight the purpose	Done
10/31/16	line objectives what they mean so employees understand.	Done

FIGURE 9.4

The customized work system map at Lifetime Products includes additional sections for Lean tools, training, and auditing.

Improvement System:	Systems Development	WS Leader:	Nate McConkie

Work System Purpose

-Develop Business Systems, Work Systems and other resources in order to cultivate a culture of continuous improvement for all employees that leads to right behavior and right results.

- Develop system leaders so that they will be able to effectively implement and execute the elements of a system.

Line Item Objectives

1. Assess/Review Work Systems in order to to coach leaders, align resources, and create a culture of improvement
2. Help BSG, BS and WS leaders develop and implement effectively the 8 elements of the work systems.
3. Provide effective resources to Business System and Work System leaders in the form of Mentoring and Trainings
4. Align Work Systems with Lifetime Improvement Plan.

Measurements / Formulas

Measurements	Formulas
Qtrly WS Assessments (2,3,4) (BS Chart)	Total Assessments completed per qtr / 78 (Goal:100%)
Quarterly BSG Reviews Completed	# of completed / Total BSG (Goal : 4)
Company Kaizens (4)	Total Kaizen per month / 1 Kaizen per employee (12/Year)
Review Business System Initiatives (4)	1 Review per map per quarter (Goal: 18 / Qtr)
Kaizen Participation by Area	Kaizen Dashboard

Terms Key

BSG= Business System Group
BS= Business System
WS= Work System

Lean Tools

Standardized Work
Coaching
Kaizen
PDCA
Visual / 5S
Problem Solving

Standard Work	Quantity	Reports
Work System Assessment Forms *		Business System Chart***
Work System Review Form		Work System Review Form *
WS Map Template		Work System Assessment Data *
BS Standard Work		Communication Board
Lean Tour Standard Work		Kaizen Dashboard - Coaching Tool

Training Plan		Auditing Plan	User
BS leader / WS leader Training	Semi-Annual	WS Assessments	Quarterly
New WS leader Training	As needed	Standard Worl	Monthly
Assessments/Review Training	As Needed	Business System Group Review	Quarterly
BS Standard Work	Quarterly		
Kaizen Training	Annual		

Monthly Measurements

Leader	User
Nate McConkie	BS Group Leaders
	BS Leaders
	WS Leaders

7/26/21

Date	Work System Action Log	Status
11/14/18	Re-write the purpose to more clearly state my goals	
11/14/18	Re-write the line item objectives using the new purpose	
11/14/18	Update measurements to reflect the line item objectives - Think through what	
11/14/18	Update training section eliminating items not corresponding to systems	
11/14/18	List only lean tools that are used in the system (Not just a picture of the house of	
11/14/18	Decide if there are other lean tools that I need to train to system leaders not	
02/15/15	Improve review/assessment assignments by having BS leaders select carefully their assessor upstream or downstream intentionally	
02/15/15	Consider having executive do one of the quarterlies with the WS Leaders - DWs	
02/15/15	Formalize training schedule for WS leaders	
02/15/15	Visit OC Tanner	
02/15/15	Consider having outside companies tour Lifetime and gather their input and	
03/13/20	Added Annual Kaizen Training to the training section.	
03/13/20	Added Kaizen Participation by Area as a Measurement	

FIGURE 9.5

An improvement sub-system map from Lifetime Products. Notice that the improvement log is placed to the side of the main map.

Management System: Product Development

Managment Systems Owner: Mitch Johnson

Goal or Objective:	Measurements	
Develop innovative quality new products that drive growth and make money. Develop a team passionate about developing innovative, highly-valued products that meet and anticipate the needs of our customers. Design, engineer, test, and iterate our products to continually increase value to the customer.	PD Sales % of Total Sales	1
	PD Gross Margin %	2
	PD Ship on time	3
	R&D Budget performance	4
	Kaizen's per employee per month	5
	Time to Market	6

Line Item Objectives:

Design Innovative(patent,growth,profit) product that anticipates customer desires and exceeds expectation.

Continually improve product designs to add value by reducing cost of materials, manufacturing and service as well as increase customer satisfaction.

Effectively communicate design objectives to the company and suppliers so they can produce goods that meet the design intent.

Ship new product on time and respect the lead time of down stream development operations.

Maintain accurate information about product so the company can effectively plan, purchase raw materials, manufacture, distribute and service the product.

Create a respectful work enviroment that fosters creativity and innovation as well as motivation to excel.

Work Systems	Work System Goal or Objective	Owner
Design	Enable design of innovative product while meeting desired specifications. Optimizes use of CAD and other technologies.	Mitch
Product Category Management	Integrate Sales, Marketing and R&D to drive category growth and profit. Work as a team to engage the company in making product development successful.	Dave W
Change/BOM Management	Implement changes to product timely and accurately. Take the engineer's design and produce a BOM that enables purchasing and production to produce the item.	Antonio Cavallo
CAD Mgt	Users will have the necessary training, hardware, and software required to create, view, and mark-up CAD models and drawings per company requirements.	Brady
Project Management	Manage projects by using approved templates designed to share critical information, prioritize projects to optimize resources and meet critical dates.	Shelly Gardiner
Testing	Develop and execute test plans to validate product design.	Lance Bosgeiter
Employee Development	Cultivate and develop a passionate team.	Lance Bosgeiter

FIGURE 9.6

The Lifetime Products management system map includes the relevant work system aim (labeled "goal or objective").

Work System Assessment Form__User Level

Work System:	Who is being assessed:
Assessment Team:	Date:

Work System

0-2 [ ] Can you please show where your work system map is posted/located

Lifetime Improvement Plan

0-2 [ ] Can you please show the 2020-2021 Lifetime Improvement Plan

Work System Purpose

0-2 [ ] What is purpose of your work system?

Work System Objectives

0-2 [ ] What are the objectives of your work system?

0-2 [ ] What do you do to personally support the work system objectives?

Measurements w/formulas

0-2 [ ] Company Measurements: Give 2 examples of company measurements that you directly affect.

0-2 [ ] Work System Measurements: How frequently are the work system measurements reviewed with you?

Standard Work

0-2 [ ] What Standard Work do you follow in this work system? Show 2 examples.

System Tools or Reports

0-2 [ ] Which System Tools or Reports do you use in this work system? Show 2 examples

Improvement

0-2 [ ] Show and explain your Kaizen Board or equivalent.

0-2 [ ] Give an example of a kaizen you have completed.

Lean tools

0-2 [ ] Please give 2 examples of visual workplace /5S in the work system area.

0-2 [ ] Referring to the house of lean from the Lifetime improvement plan, explain 2 lean tools you Kaizen, Standard Work and Visual/5S.

FIGURE 9.7

An important part of creating an organization that thinks systemically is regularly auditing formalized systems. Lifetime Products has a very formal assessment form.

Training Plan

0-2 [ ] Please explain what training you have received for this work system.

Auditing Plan

0-2 [ ] Have you performed an audit in the last 3 months? (examples could include auditing an element in the work

system or auditing your own role in the work system)

Lifetime Improvement Plan

Explain the following:

0-2 [ ] What is Lifetimes mission statement?

0-2 [ ] Principles: Give 2 examples of Lifetime principles, and how you use them in your area?

0-2 [ ] Initiatives: Give 2 examples of initiatives that you directly affect?

Principles

0-2 [ ] How is ideal behavior recognized for your area at Lifetime? (Principles)

0-2 [ ] How does your area address any questions, needs, suggestions or improvements you might have?

0-2 [ ] Tell us one thing we can do to improve this work system.

[ ] Total Score (Out of 42)

Guidance to Assessors and Mentors: This assessment is designed to take 30 min

-The employee chosen for the User Level Assessment needs to be picked at random with minimal notice

-This assessment is intended to ensure/measure ideal behavior (in order to get ideal results)

-The assessment should include the Mentor, Assessor, and the user being assessed (WS Leader can be Mentor)

-The mentor & assessor can ask questions modified to the user as needed to assess understanding/behavior

Role of a User within the Work System:

- Understand what parts of the Work System apply to them • Execute their responsibility in the Work System • Improve the Work System (driven by system)

Work System & Assessment

A Work System provides necessary tools, direction, and resources to drive improvement. The it promotes standard work, helps organize content, and articulates objectives. **The Work System is being assessed, not the user.**

FIGURE 9.7

(Continued)

Documents: The work system review is an Excel form with questions to be discussed by the reviewer(s) and the work system leader. Any action items are added to the improvement log portion of the work system map by the reviewer and assigned to the work system leader (Figure 9.8).

For the first few years, system maps were assessed regularly with 23 scored questions that an assessment team would pose to people working in the system to be assessed. The assessment would be scheduled ahead of time. The score and formal nature of the assessment led to high levels of anxiety for the workers being assessed, so Lifetime Products recently introduced a second option in which questions focused on the components of the system are more open-ended and are not scored. In this review, the goal is to generate action items for an improvement log.

Work System Review Form__User Level		
Work System:	**Owner:**	
Review Team (1 reviewer required):		**Date:**

The goal of the Work System review is to generate action items leading to improvement.

Please ask at least one question from each section to drive discussion about the work system.

Use of Work System Map

The work system map is a great communication tool available to direct the work performed within an area.

How often do you use the Work System content?

How does the Work System Map providing a forum for communication of purpose/goal/tools and results?

How could the communication flow be improved (Upward communication or downward communication)?

Work System Purpose

The Work System Purpose needs to clearly articulate the exact purpose of the system. This statement becomes the mission of the system and needs to be shared with the users.

What is there in the purpose that does not align with the work you do each day?

How would you explain your Work System purpose to someone outside you area?

How does the purpose help clarify why you come to work each day? How does it provide vision for your area?

Line Item Objectives

Line Item Objectives break apart the Work System Purpose and further define objectives so users can better understand the Work System Purpose. (What and Why...not How)

What line item objectives do you you not fully understand?

What do you do in your work that doesn't tie into the objectives?

Which objective do you think is most important to your success? Why is it the most important?

Measurements w/formulas

The measurements should show how well the system is achieving its objectives. Each Line item objective should have a measurement(s) that indicates objective performance. Measurements need to be reviewed on a regular basis with the system users to drive improvement and to see how well the system is working.

How are measurements shared within your area? (Monthly meeting, communication board, emailed...) How could this be improved?

How often do you think the measurements should be shared with the members? How often are they shared? If there are differences what do you think could close the gap?

What value do you receive from review of measurements?

Which measurement is your favorite and why?

FIGURE 9.8

Lifetime Products Work System Review form.

Standard Work

Standard Work refers to any documented process. It is key to system performance and improvement.

Can you show me where the Standard Work is for your job duties?

Tell me about a Kaizen you have submitted to improve the Standard Work in your area.

A) Do you feel Standard Work covers all areas of your work responsibility? If not, what needs to be added?

B) Is there any process that is hard or feels unsafe to perform? What could we do to improve it?

System Tools or Reports

System reports are a list of documents that are used to meet the Line Item Objectives. Reports are created as needed to be used within the system.

Show me where your tools or reports are located?

How were you trained on the reports/tools?

Which report or tool do you wish you better understood? Why?

Which tool/report is most useful in your area? Why?

Lean tools

This is a list of lean tools from the Lifetime House of Lean that are being utilized within the system.

Tell me about a Kaizen you have submitted within the last 3 months.

What Lean Tool do you wish you understood better? (You may have to show them the house of lean to let them know what options are available) Why?

Which Lean Tool is most useful in your area (other than Kaizen)? Why?

Training Plan

The training plan outlines how Standard Work, Reports, and Lean Tools are to be trained to all users of the system.

Approximately what % of the tools/reports/standard works have you been trained to perform/use?

How is training tracked in your area?

How often do you think the team members in your area could use training?

Auditing Plan

An auditing process is key to improving the execution side of the system. Audits refer to internal inspections of the system: Work System Assessments, Standard Work, Reports, Lean Tools, etc.

How do you make sure you are doing your job correctly (according to the standard work)?

Are you aware of any audits being performed to ensure that the team is following the correct processes?

What opportunities are there to perform more audits, or get credit for audits already happening, in your area/WS?

Wrap Up

1- Reviewer needs to document the action items on the action log next to the work system

2 - Work system Leader is responsible for the completion of the action items. Follow up will happen on the next review.

3 - Reviewer will need to reach out to the WS Leader to let them know that action items have been added.

FIGURE 9.8
(Continued)

When given the choice, most system leaders prefer the second, more friendly approach.

LESSONS LEARNED AT O.C. TANNER AND LIFETIME PRODUCTS

Every organization will approach implementation of System Design a little differently. Following is a comparison of implementation by organization.

- Lifetime Products focused on work systems first. O.C. Tanner focused on improvement sub-systems first.

- Lifetime Products uses customized maps. O.C. Tanner chose to make no customizations to the Shingo system maps until after they had used them for a while.
- Lifetime Products and O.C. Tanner take a different approach to reviewing the systems. Lifetime Products implemented both an assessment and a review process. O.C. Tanner asks system leaders to share their work on maps, their one-page summary, and PowerPoint presentation with other leaders and tour visitors.
- Both Lifetime Products and O.C. Tanner recognize that completing and reviewing the system maps leads to meaningful discussion of system components.
- Both Lifetime Products and O.C. Tanner discovered that completing system maps helped them to define systems in their respective organizations.

10

Results

The five diamonds of the *Shingo Model* are Principles, Systems, Tools, Results, and Culture (Figure 10.1). System design is connected to each of the diamonds. The first Insight of Organizational Excellence states: "ideal results require ideal behaviors." The results of an organization depend on the behavior of each person. The second insight tells us that "purpose and systems drive behavior," and the third insight teaches that "principles inform ideal behavior."*

KEY PERFORMANCE INDICATORS

The Key Performance Indicators (KPIs) are the basic measurements or metrics of an organization. They are measures of how well an organization is achieving its purpose. KPIs measure ideal results whether or not the ideal is achieved. The Shingo Institute has a list of potential measurements in its Shingo Prize application. A list of about 50 possible measurements is available in the results section of the Shingo Assessment Guidelines,[†] which is published for those organizations interested in challenging for the Shingo Prize. Table 10.1 shows the strongly recommended measures.

KEY BEHAVIORAL INDICATORS

Key Behavioral Indicators (KBIs) are what we need to do to improve the performance measurements. KBIs measure ideal behaviors.

---

* Shingo Institute, *The Shingo Model*, 10.
† Shingo Institute, *Shingo Assessment Guidelines* (Logan, UT: Shingo Institute, 2020), 13–14.

DOI: 10.4324/9781003267768-10

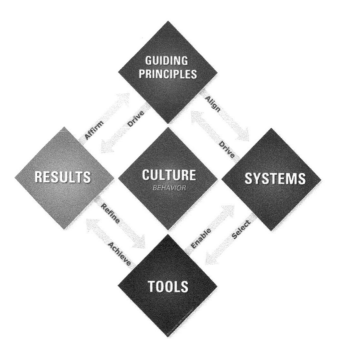

FIGURE 10.1
The *Shingo Model.*

Unfortunately, many organizations overlook key behavioral indicators. As leading indicators are completely dependent on individual humans, KBIs may be difficult to name because they are based on human behavior. Organizational results depend upon behavior, so an organization striving for excellence must carefully consider behavior. According to Morgan Jones, lead assessor at BHP Billiton Group Operations in Melbourne, Australia, and a Shingo Publication Award recipient author, carefully considering people's behavior can positively impact KPIs. He says, "The results come. Instead of always focusing on dollars and savings, it's about focus on the people, external people—our customers—and internal staff. That drives the culture, that drives the results."*

Properly selected key behavioral indicators of a particular system (i.e., what you list in that section of the system design map) can forecast successes or weaknesses that will show up later on in the performance measures. Thus, KBIs are leading metrics.

---

* Gerhard Plenert, ed., *Discover Excellence: An Overview of the Shingo Model and Its Guiding Principles* (Boca Raton, FL: CRC Press, 2018), 74.

Shingo Results Measures	
Safety, Environment, Morale Number of ideas per employee and degree of employee idea implementation Near-misses (safety) Survey (measure of employee trust and confidence in organization and management) Employee turnover **Financial/Cost/Productivity** Productivity of cash (cash flow) Key value stream margins Inventory Turns (organizational raw, working, and finished inventories)	**Delivery** On-time delivery complete to customer by request date Total lead time (the time from customer order to customer receipt) Processing cycle time **Quality** Quality to the customer (defect-free delivery) Finished product first pass yield and/or rework **Customer Satisfaction** Market share Customer surveys

TABLE 10.1

A listing of the Shingo Institute's strongly recommended measures (KPIs) appear in the "Achievement Report for Challenging for Shingo Prize: Results"

MEASURES AND PEOPLE

Measurements are important to clearly understand where the organization is and where it is going. They are not generally effective as motivation. In fact, according to Alfie Kohn, author of *Punished by Rewards*, the more we try to motivate people with rewards or incentives, the more harm we can do. Consider this succinct summary of some of Kohn's work from the book section of his website:

> *Drawing from hundreds of studies, Kohn demonstrates that people actually do inferior work when they are enticed with money, grades, or other incentives. Programs that use rewards to change people's behavior are similarly ineffective over the long run. Promising goodies to children for good behavior can never produce anything more than temporary obedience. In fact, the more we use artificial inducements to motivate people, the more they lose interest in what we're bribing them to do. Rewards turn play into work, and work into drudgery.**

---

* Alfie Kohn, "Punished by Rewards," accessed April 7, 2021, https://www.alfiekohn.org/punished -rewards/.

Because a measurement is the result of the behaviors of many people, it can be a mistake to assign accountability for a measurement to an individual person. It is better to assign accountability for a measurement to a team. An individual who is assigned the accountability for a measurement may feel that they are being blamed for poor performance. Blaming an individual for a team measurement is ineffective, but extremely common.

While we win or lose as a team, we must coach individual behavior. The great football coaches know that. At the end of the game, they have won or lost as a team. But when preparing for the game, they coach individual positions—what each individual needs to do to contribute to the team's victory. When evaluating key performance indicators, a team scorecard is a good way to provide feedback. Key behavioral indicators are individual, so a list of individual behaviors is the way to give feedback.

Most team members are self-motivated, what Deming calls "pride of workmanship."[*] Measurements are effective at informing a team about how it is doing. However, it is the behaviors of each person that creates the actual improvement. Behaviors can be practiced without being measured. We need to encourage deliberate practice[†] with as little pressure as possible. In a business environment, we are all concerned about the performance of the business. But we need to create an off-line practice environment to learn new skills. This is particularly important for new workers. They should be allowed to observe the work and practice the work before they are expected to perform the work with exactness.

IDEAL RESULTS

When we discuss ideal results, we cannot look solely at KPIs and assume we have the complete picture. Ideal results require a foundation of KBIs. While the first insight from the *Shingo Model* tells us "ideal results require ideal behavior," it is unusual to shift a culture from current state to ideal behavior immediately. The gap between ideal behavior and current practice is usually too large. In fact, the ideal behavior is the end goal and may

---

[*] W. Edwards Deming, *Out of the Crisis*, 72.

[†] The phrase "deliberate practice" was introduced to the editors by Billy Taylor, a leading management improvement expert. See Billy Taylor, "Deliberate Practice: Optimizing Daily Management Systems" (Keynote address, 32nd Annual Shingo Conference, October 13, 2020).

never be perfectly achieved. (Perfect achievement of ideal behavior would be the correct people intensely practicing the correct behavior all the time throughout the organization.) Striving to evolve the indicator (KBI) closer to the ideal behavior will lead to more accuracy in your ability to predict the result (KPI). As KPIs change and become more challenging, KBIs may also need to change to meet the challenge.

Ideal results need to be understandable and measurable throughout an organization. Ultimately, team members need to feel that they can influence and predict performance results (KPIs) through improving the necessary behaviors (KBIs) that lead to the outcomes being measured.

11

System Thinking

The Shingo system design approach was developed as a practical application of systems thinking as taught by three important scholars: Peter Senge, Russell Ackoff, and W. Edwards Deming. Following is a brief overview of their thinking that has been most influential in the development of the Shingo Institute's recommendations included in this book.

PETER SENGE

Peter Senge, a senior lecturer at the MIT-Sloane School of Management and founder of the Society for Organizational Learning, wrote *The Fifth Discipline: The Art and Practice of the Learning Organization*.

Some relevant thoughts from Peter Senge:

> *The first principle of systems thinking: structure influences behavior. When placed in the same system, people, however different, tend to produce similar results.**

It is essential to implement organizational structures that support the behaviors that lead to desired results. Organizing all components, including the five required communication tools, into a system map specific to each of the three essential types of systems is a method the Shingo Institute recommends to create the structure.

---

* Peter Senge, *The Fifth Discipline: The Art and Practice of the Learning Organization* (New York: Doubleday, 1990), 42.

DOI: 10.4324/9781003267768-11   *117*

> *System thinking is a discipline for seeing wholes. It is a framework for seeing interrelationships rather than things, seeing patterns of change rather than static "snapshots."**

The system maps are literally designed to help you see the whole. The suggested regimen of scheduled feedback—ideally given in person—and improvement log records are two ways that people in your organization will become aware of patterns of change. While a system map may present a periodic static snapshot for review, it is intended to be a dynamic, ever-changing, living document that illuminates patterns of change.

> *In fact, sadly, for most people "system thinking" means "fighting complexity with complexity," devising increasingly "complex" (we should really say "detailed") solutions to increasingly "complex" problems. In fact, this is the antithesis of real system thinking.*†

The system map is intended to be simple and to facilitate simple, natural conversations by getting an organization on the same page (literally).

> *The essence of mastering systems thinking as a management discipline lies in seeing patterns where others see only events and forces to react to.*‡

Our patterns of system thinking:

1. Each organization needs to agree upon the definition of a "system." If we call everything a system, then nothing is a system.
2. Organizations need to transform an existing informal structure consisting of processes, programs, tools, and measurements that are loosely connected into a tight system structure consisting of three essential systems and the five required communication tools.
3. The tool we use to create this tight structure is the system map.

---

* Senge, *The Fifth Discipline*, 68.
† Senge, *The Fifth Discipline*, 72.
‡ Senge, *The Fifth Discipline*, 126.

4. System maps need to be reviewed on a scheduled cadence to drive improvement.

Additional relevant quotes from Peter Senge can be found in Appendix A.

RUSSELL ACKOFF

Russell Ackoff, emeritus professor of Management Science in the Wharton School of Business at the University of Pennsylvania, was a pioneer in the field of operations research, systems thinking, and management science. He taught:

> *If we have a system of improvement that is directed at improving the parts taken separately, you can be absolutely sure that the performance of the whole will not be improved. ... But most applications of improvement programs are directed at improving the parts taken separately. Not the whole.**

The Shingo system design approach formalizes systems in order to better connect the elements of the systems to capitalize on Ackoff's teaching that the performance of the system depends on how the parts fit together, not how each part acts on its own.

Ackoff explains that all parts are interconnected.

> *A system is a whole, that consists of parts, each of which can affect its behavior or its properties. ... Each part of the system, when it affects the system, is dependent on its affect from some other part. In other words, the parts are interdependent. No part of a system, or collection of parts of a system, has an independent effect on it. ... The parts are all interconnected.†*

---

* Russell Ackoff, "Beyond Continual Improvement," 1994. YouTube video, 12:18, https://www.youtube.com/watch?v=OqEeIG8aPPk. Start at 5:23.

† https://www.youtube.com/watch?v=OqEeIG8aPPk starting at 3:40.

In our experience, it is not simply the connection, but the quality of the connection that is most important. The purpose of the system maps is to create what we call "tight connections."

He illustrates as follows:

> *The essential or defining properties of any system are properties of the whole, which none of its parts have. For example, a very elementary system you are all familiar with is an automobile. The essential property of an automobile is that it can carry you from one place to another. No part of an automobile can do that—the wheel can't, the axel can't, the seat can't, the motor can't. The motor can't even carry itself from one place to another. But the automobile can.**

The only way to get a functioning automobile is when the parts are connected.

The approach presented in this book acknowledges and applies the importance of interdependent parts. The five required communication tools are necessary to ensure tight connections within the system. As Ackoff taught: "The system is not the sum of the behavior of its parts, it is the product of its interactions."† When you use the system maps to see the whole of your system, you will find that interactions become apparent. The system maps presented in this book exist to assist you in seeing the whole of your system in one place, on one page.

W. EDWARDS DEMING

The third thought leader is W. Edwards Deming, who is best known for his pioneering work in the 1950s in Japan where he taught methods for improving how top managers and engineers worked and learned together.‡ His contribution to system thinking is based on his books *Out of the Crisis* and *The New Economics for Industry, Government, Education.*

---

* https://www.youtube.com/watch?v=OqEeIG8aPPk starting at 4:05.
† https://www.youtube.com/watch?v=OqEeIG8aPPk starting at 5:16.
‡ The Deming Institute, "Deming the Man."

Deming taught: "Any substantial improvement must come from action on the system, the responsibility of management."*

In his book *Out of the Crisis*, Deming gives 14 Points for the Transformation of Management First. (A complete list of Deming's points can be found in Appendix B.) The following four points are particularly relevant to system thinking:

- It is management's responsibility to create a constancy of purpose (Point 1)
- Institute leadership (Point 7)
- Drive out fear (Point 8)
- Break down barriers between departments (Point 9)

Management's Responsibility: Constancy of Purpose

When applied to systems, constancy of purpose means that everyone in the organization is aligned to the aim of the organization through a formal structure that is needed to enforce the disciplined behaviors needed to reach the goals and objective of the organization. A manager working in an organization with well-defined and functioning formal systems will spend less time responding to immediate emergencies and more time developing and improving systems and system leaders. System maps provide a structured approach to document, create, and maintain constancy of purpose for the organization.

Institute Leadership

The management system map provides a disciplined structure for developing leaders. At all levels of the organization, system maps provide a simple, formal method for developing leadership by clearly communicating the current state of systems as well as the leaders' responsibilities for improving them.

Drive Out Fear

Because most workers take pride in their work, a common fear is criticism from supervisors and peers. Deming observed: "It is not enough to do

---

* Deming, *Out of the Crisis*, 7, 24–26.

your best; you must know what to do, and then do your best."* System maps provide the structure for people to understand exactly what they should do and how to do it. When systems make people feel safe, improved performance follows.

The *Shingo Model* booklet states: "Systems drive the behavior of people, or rather they create the conditions that cause people to behave in a certain way. We have to create systems where people feel safe."[†]

Break Down Barriers Between Departments

The Shingo system design approach encourages breaking down barriers by establishing common language and definitions (your organization's glossary). People working within a system will use the five required communication tools in similar ways. Management systems create an opportunity for work and improvement system leaders to communicate regularly. Properly functioning management systems will break down barriers and help the whole organization.

As you put the theory of system thinking into practice, you will begin designing systems in a way that will drive behavior toward the ideal leading to new levels of performance.

RESISTANCE TO CHANGE

As you design the systems of your organization, transforming your informal systems into the formal systems, it will be normal for you to experience some resistance. It has been observed that different people react and adapt to change in different ways. Luckily, a group's reaction to change is predictable. Figure 11.1 shows how you can expect your organization to adapt to innovations[‡] like formalizing systems. As your organization begins to think systemically, you can expect to experience these stages of adoption.

---

* The W. Edwards Deming Institute, "Quote by W. Edwards Deming."
† Shingo Institute. *The Shingo Model*, 14.
‡ Everett M. Rogers, *Diffusion of Innovations* (New York, NY: Free Press of Glencoe, 1972).

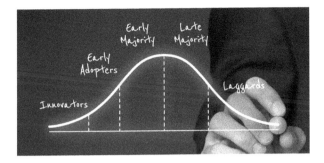

FIGURE 11.1
Recognizing the stages of adopting change at your own organization will help you prepare for successfully integrating system thinking.

You might find it helpful to predict how the people in your organization will respond to the innovations provided by system design. The following questions can guide your thinking:

- What are the advantages of being an early adopter?
- What are the disadvantages of being an early adopter?
- How do you manage each group of adopters?

While you need early adopters to champion the benefits of formalized systems, not everyone needs to be an early adopter. Early adopters make mistakes and bring to light the customizations that your organization will need to adapt systems design and make it your own. In the beginning of your system design journey, creating four to five maps per quarter is a good pace. Those involved in these first system maps will be the early adopters working to define the format and terminology, create a glossary, see what works, and discover what doesn't work. It is wise to limit the number of people involved in the beginning to prevent wasting resources in this groundbreaking, experimental stage. Start with people who are willing and excited about the benefits of formalized systems. Have them start small and take one step at a time. Be sure to celebrate the early successes even as you work to smooth the future adoption throughout your organization. Be sure to listen to the concerns of the early adopters and those who are more hesitant. Your implementation plan should evolve and increase in scope.

System design can change the behavior of the people within your organization. When behavior changes, culture changes. Changing your organization's culture by embedding the behaviors of thinking systemically will result in increased connections, collaboration, communication, alignment, and consistency of execution.

PUTTING IT ALL TOGETHER

The original definition of a system given by W. Edward Deming states*: "A system is a network of interdependent components that work together to try to accomplish the aim of the system." Deming's phrase "a network of interdependent components" means that the strength of the system is determined by the strength of the connections between the components (Figure 11.2).

Let's look at the connections between the systems diamond and the rest of the model. Systems provide the structure that drives the desired

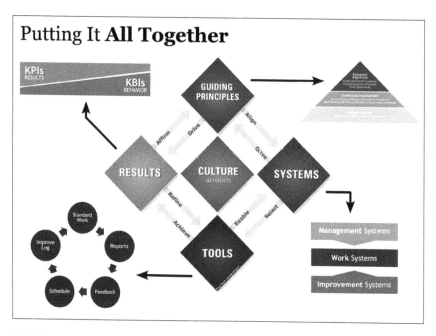

FIGURE 11.2
The three essential systems and five required communication tools are an integral part of the *Shingo Model*.

---

* Deming, *The New Economics*, 50.

behavior. Principle-based systems aligned to ideal behavior will drive behavior ever closer to the ideal. Selected tools enable a system to achieve results.

To be a formal system, an organization must incorporate all five communication tools. Formalized systems focus on both results and the behaviors that achieve them. Results measure system performance. Systems and tools tell us who, what, where, when, and how. Principles tell us why.

SYSTEMS DRIVE BEHAVIORS

Important insights from the *Shingo Model* are found on page 10 of *The Shingo Model* booklet (Figure 11.3). These three insights provide a good summary of how the *Shingo Model* diamonds are connected.

1. Ideal Results Require Ideal Behaviors

   The results of an organization depend on the way its people behave. To achieve ideal results, leaders must do the hard work of creating a

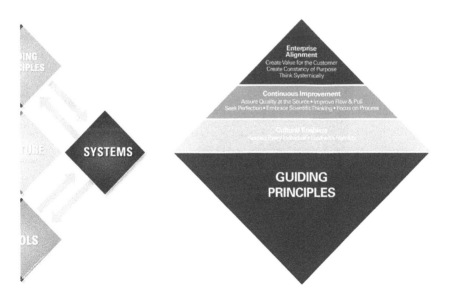

FIGURE 11.3
Principles inform ideal behavior in all systems.

principles-based culture where ideal behaviors are expected and evident in every team member.

2. Purpose and Systems Drive Behavior

    Managers have an enormous task to align management, improvement, and work systems to drive the ideal behavior required by all people to achieve ideal business results.

3. Principles Inform Ideal Behavior

    The more deeply one understands principles, the more clearly he or she understands ideal behavior. The more clearly one understands ideal behavior, the better he or she can design systems to drive that behavior to achieve ideal results.

As you can tell, we consider the *Shingo Model* essential to reaping all of the benefits of formalized systems (Figure 11.4). You can find a copy of the *Model* booklet at the Shingo Institute website at https://shingo.org/shingo -model/.

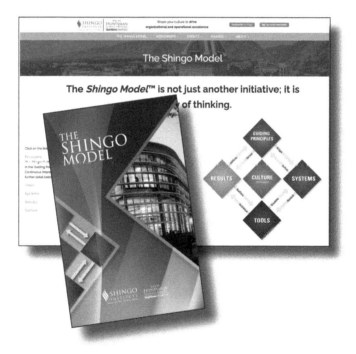

FIGURE 11.4

A free copy of *The Shingo Model* booklet can be downloaded from the Shingo Institute website.

This book was written to support and expand on the ideas presented in the Shingo SYSTEM DESIGN workshop. The personal interactions and host site experience of applying system design are invaluable. You can register for a workshop on the Shingo Institute website at https://shingo .org/education/.

CREATING A SYSTEM MAPS PROJECT

Now that you have a vision of what system design can bring to your organization, we recommend that you create a formal project plan. Here are our recommendations for how to get started:

- Identify a project leader.
- Identify the project team members.
- Decide the meeting cadence (weekly, bi-weekly, etc.).
- Create a three-month schedule to formalize three work systems, two improvement sub-systems, and one management system.
- Create an organization-specific systems glossary.
- Create training for your new formalized systems.

FINAL THOUGHTS

As we conclude this book, we hope that you understand how to create maps to formalize the work, improvement, and management systems in your organization. We hope that the value of the five essential communication tools is clear. It has been our experience that inviting the people of an organization to carefully discuss and define their systems is the first step to cultivating systems that will drive behaviors toward excellence.

Appendix A: Quotes from Peter Senge's *The Fifth Discipline**

At the heart of learning organizations is a shift of mind—from seeing ourselves as separate from the world to connected to the world, some seeing problems as caused by someone or something "out there" to seeing how our own actions create the problems we experience. (Page 12)

The first principle of systems thinking: structure influences behavior. When placed in the same system, people, however different, tend to produce similar results. (Page 42)

For systems thinking also shows that small, well focused actions can sometimes produce significant, enduring improvements, if they're in the right place. System thinking refers to this principle as leverage. (Page 64)

System thinking is a discipline for seeing wholes. It is a framework for seeing interrelationships rather than things, seeing patterns of change rather than static "snapshots." (Page 68)

System thinking offers a language that begins by restructuring how we think. (Page 69)

In fact, sadly, for most people "system thinking" means "fighting complexity with complexity," devising increasingly "complex" (we should really say "detailed") solutions to increasingly "complex" problems. In fact, this is the antithesis of real system thinking. (Page 72)

In mastering system thinking, we give up the assumption that there is an individual, or individual agent, responsible. The feedback perspective suggests that everyone shares responsibility for problems generated by a system. (Page 78)

---

* Senge, *The Fifth Discipline.*

In fact, the essence of mastering systems thinking as a management discipline lies in seeing patterns where others see only events and forces to react to. (Page 124)

Appendix B: W. Edwards Deming's 14 Points for the Transformation of Management First*

1. Create constancy of purpose toward improvement of product and service, with the aim to become competitive and to stay in business, and to provide jobs.
2. Adopt the new philosophy. We are in a new economic age. Western management must awaken to the challenge, must learn their responsibilities, and take on leadership for change.
3. Cease dependence on inspection to achieve quality. Eliminate the need for inspection on a mass basis by building quality into the product in the first place.
4. End the practice of awarding business on the basis of price tag. Instead, minimize total cost. Move toward a single supplier for any one item, on a long-term relationship of loyalty and trust.
5. Improve constantly and forever the system of production and service, to improve quality and productivity, and thus constantly decrease costs.
6. Institute training on the job.
7. Institute leadership. The aim of supervision should be to help people and machines and gadgets to do a better job. Supervision of management is in need of overhaul, as well as supervision of production workers.
8. Drive out fear, so that everyone may work effectively for the company.
9. Break down barriers between departments. People in research, design, sales, and production must work as a team, to foresee

---

* As presented in Dr. Deming's classic book, *Out of the Crisis*, 23–24.

problems of production and in use that may be encountered with the product or service.

10. Eliminate slogans, exhortations, and targets for the work force asking for zero defects and new levels of productivity. Such exhortations only create adversarial relationships, as the bulk of the causes of low quality and low productivity belong to the system and thus lie beyond the power of the work force.

11a. Eliminate work standards (quotas) on the factory floor. Substitute leadership.

11b. Eliminate management by objective. Eliminate management by numbers, numerical goals. Substitute leadership.

12a. Remove barriers that rob the hourly worker of his right to pride of workmanship. The responsibility of supervisors must be changed from sheer numbers to quality.

12b. Remove barriers that rob people in management and in engineering of their right to pride of workmanship. This means, *inter alia*, abolishment of the annual or merit rating and of management by objective.

13. Institute a vigorous program of education and self-improvement.

14. Put everybody in the company to work to accomplish the transformation. The transformation is everybody's job.

Glossary

Aim: The direction or purpose of a system.

Cadence: The frequency of feedback in a system.

Components: A part or element of a larger whole. In a system, components include a system name, system leader, aim, workflow (in a work system), team members, improvement sub-systems (in work and management systems), standard work, reports, feedback, schedules, improvement log, and results (KPIs and KBIs).

Constancy of Purpose: A clear understanding, by everyone in the organization, of the organization's aim and what needs to be done to achieve that aim. Constancy of purpose is the first of W. Edwards Deming's 14 points.

Culture: All of the behaviors within an organization.

Dimensions: The Guiding Principles diamond in the *Shingo Model* is divided into three categories of ideal behaviors: Cultural Enablers, Continuous Improvement, and Enterprise Alignment. These categories, or dimensions, are also referred to as people, process, and purpose.

Feedback: One of five required system communication tools. The feedback tool is a review of a system and its components, written or verbal, by either an internal or external member. See also *system communication tools.*

Ideal Behavior: Actions (behavior) that create outcomes that produce results and are both excellent and sustainable.

Ideal Result: Outcomes that are aligned, that are both excellent and sustainable, and that demonstrate improvement over time.

Improvement Log: One of five required system communication tools. The improvement log is a document that captures system improvement ideas and assignments. See also *system communication tools.*

Improvement System: One of three essential systems in the Systems diamond of the *Shingo Model.* The improvement system focuses on making the organization better and is made up of various sub-systems. See also *system.*

Insights of Organizational Excellence: Three important truths that help guide organizations as they embrace the *Shingo Model* and its guiding principles during their cultural transformations. The three insights are: (1) Ideal Results Require Ideal Behavior, (2) Purpose and Systems Drive Behavior, and (3) Principles Inform Ideal Behavior.

Key Behavioral Indicators (KBI): Measurements that track behaviors. KBIs should be predictive indicators of Key Performance Indicator (KPI) outcomes. Key behavior indicators are also what we measure behaviorally to determine whether or not the organization is moving closer to ideal behavior.

Key Performance Indicator (KPI): Key metrics that are traditionally used by organizations to measure performance, such as sales/revenue or income/net profit. KPIs are a measure of what the culture has been able to achieve. See also *result.*

Management System: One of three essential systems in the Systems diamond of the *Shingo Model.* Management systems focus on leading the organization by developing system leaders. See also *system.*

Organizational Excellence: A constantly changing and evolving state in which an organization moves closer to excellence as it achieves its desired results as an outcome of behaviors. These behaviors are driven by systems that can sustain not only the results but also the culture that created them.

Principle: A foundational rule that is universal and timeless, evident, and that governs consequences.

Reports: One of five required system communication tools. Reports are information or data used to make decisions and to complete work. See also *system communication tools.*

Result: A measurable outcome. See also *key performance indicator.*

Schedule: One of five required system communication tools. A schedule is a cadence of feedback such as meetings, reviews, and audits. See also *system communication tools.*

Shingo Model: A graphical illustration of how guiding principles, systems, tools, and results interact and connect within an organization to create organizational culture. The *Shingo Model* provides a powerful framework to enable organizations to accelerate a cultural transformation and achieve sustainable results.

Standard Work: One of five required system communication tools. Standard work is a documented sequence of the best current way to do a process. See also *system communication tools.*

Supporting Concepts: Concepts that provide additional insight into the ideal behaviors that are informed by the *Shingo Guiding Principles.* These supporting concepts are generally more familiar to practitioners and students of organizational excellence.

System: A network of interdependent components that work together to accomplish its aim. The three essential systems defined in the Systems diamond of the *Shingo Model* are work, management, and improvement systems. See also *work system, management system, improvement system.*

System Communication Tools: A single device or item that accomplishes a specific task. System communication tools include standard work, reports, feedback, schedule, and improvement log. See also *standard work, reports, feedback, schedule, improvement log.*

System Glossary: A controlled vocabulary defined by an organization and used within its systems. Because systems are designed by each organization, a glossary is a customizable tool that can provide clarity to the organization.

System Map: A spreadsheet that lists the components of a system. These components include aim, system members, standard work, reports, feedback, schedules, improvement log, and results (KPIs and KBIs).

System Members: People who are responsible for completing the work of the system. Customers of a system are not considered to be system members.

System Optimization: Collaboration, as compared to component optimization, or competition.

Workflow: The sequence of industrial, administrative, or other processes through which a piece of work passes from initiation to completion. A work system can be made up of multiple workflows that consist of many processes. Workflows are sometimes organized by job descriptions.

Work System: One of three essential systems in the Systems diamond of the *Shingo Model.* The work system focuses on workflow. A work system organizes the basic processes within an organization and can be made up of multiple workflows. See also *system.*

Bibliography

Ackoff, Russell. "Beyond Continual Improvement." Filmed 1994 at event hosted by Clare Crawford-Mason and Lloyd Dobyns. *Youtube Video*, 12:18. https://www.youtube.com/watch?v=OqEeIG8aPPk.

American Heritage Dictionaries. *American Heritage Dictionary of the English Language*, 5th edition. Boston, MA: Houghton Mifflin Harcourt Publishing Company, 2019.

Berry, Barbara. *There is a Relationship Between Systems Thinking and W. Edwards Deming's Theory of Profound Knowledge*. Tulsa, OK: The Berrywood Group, Inc., 2006.

BusinessDictionary.com. "Network." *WebFinance, Inc*, Accessed December 3, 2019. http://www.businessdictionary.com/definition/network.html.

Business Wire. "O.C. Tanner Executive Inducted into AME Hall of Fame." *Business Wire*, November 16, 2015. Accessed April 15, 2020. https://www.businesswire.com/news/home/20151116006236/en/O.C.-Tanner-Executive-Inducted-AME-Hall-Fame.

Deming Institute. "A Bad System Will Beat A Good Person Every Time." *The W. Edward Deming Institute* (blog), February 26, 2015. Accessed February 11, 2021. https://deming.org/a-bad-system-will-beat-a-good-person-every-time/.

Deming Institute. "Deming the Man." Accessed February 11, 2021. https://deming.org/deming-the-man/.

Deming Institute. "Quotes by W. Edwards Deming." Accessed April 15, 2020. https://quotes.deming.org/authors/W._Edwards_Deming/quote/10084.

Deming, W. Edwards. *Out of the Crisis*. Cambridge, MA: Massachusetts Institute of Technology, Center for Advanced Engineering Study, 1986.

Deming, W. Edwards. *The New Economics: For Industry, Government, Education*, 2nd edition. Cambridge, MA: MIT Press, 2000.

Halls, Jonathan. "Communication is Hard Work." *Jonathanhalls.com* (blog), September 14, 2017. Accessed April 15, 2021. https://jonathanhalls.com/2017/09/14/communication-is-hard-work/.

Imai, Masaaki. "What Is Kaizen?" *The Kaizen Institute Video*, 4:52. Accessed February 11, 2021. https://www.kaizen.com/what-is-kaizen.html.

Jamison, Steve and John Wooden. *Coach Wooden's Leadership Game Plan for Success: 12 Lessons for Extraordinary Performance and Personal Excellence*. New York, NY: McGraw-Hill Education, 2009.

Kohn, Alfie. "Punished by Rewards: The Trouble with Gold Stars, Incentive Plans, As, Praise, and Other Bribes." Accessed April 7, 2021. https://www.alfiekohn.org/punished-rewards/.

Linked XL. "Billy Ray Taylor – Founder & CEO: Building Success with a Servant Leader." Accessed December 7, 2020. https://linkedxl.com/our-founder/.

Miller, Robert Derald. *Hearing the Voice of the Shingo Principles: Creating Sustainable Cultures of Enterprise Excellence*. New York: Routledge, 2018.

Mumford, Troy. "Cultural Strata Effects: How Lean Culture Drivers of Engagement Vary by Employees' Level in the Organization." Speech presented at the Shingo European Conference, Copenhagen, Denmark, December 2016.

Plenert, Gerhard. *Discover Excellence: An Overview of the Shingo Model and Its Guiding Principles*. Boca Raton, FL: CRC, 2018.

Robison, Jennifer. "Turning Around Employee Turnover." *Gallup Business Journal* (May 8, 2008). Accessed April 15, 2020. https://news.gallup.com/businessjournal/106912 /turning-around-your-turnover-problem.aspx.

Rogers, Everett M. *Diffusion of Innovations*. New York: Free Press of Glencoe, 1962.

Senge, Peter M. *The Fifth Discipline: The Art and Practice of the Learning Organization*, 2nd edition. New York: Doubleday/Currency, 1990.

Shingo Institute. "Shingo Assessment Guidelines." Logan, UT: Shingo Institute, John M Huntsman School of Business, 2020. Accessed November 18, 2020. https://usu.app .box.com/s/soon7kiuivk7kdftg80zpcyz6cfh8a2b/file/667529967493.

Shingo Institute. *The Shingo Model*, version 14.6. Logan, UT: Utah State University, 2021.

Spear, Steven and Bowen, H. Kent. "Decoding the DNA of the Toyota Production System." *Harvard Business Review* vol. 77 issue 5 (Sept–Oct 1999): 96–106.

Taylor, Billy. "Deliberate Practice: Optimizing Daily Management Systems." In Keynote Address, 32nd Annual Shingo Conference, October 13, 2020.

Wile, Kris. "Peter Senge Introduction to Systems Thinking." *Video*, 2:21, September 13, 2011. Accessed April 15, 2020. https://www.youtube.com/watch?v=eXdzKBWDraM.

Womack, J. P. et al. *The Machine That Changed the World: The Story of Lean Production Toyota's Secret Weapon in the Global Car Wars That Is Now Revolutionizing World Industry*. New York: Simon & Schuster, Inc., 1990.

Index